The Poetry of Ben Jonson

By the same author

THE FLIGHTY HORSE

(Poems)

The Poetry of
Ben Jonson

J. G. NICHOLS

NEW YORK
BARNES & NOBLE, INC.

First published in Great Britain 1969
Published in the United States of America 1969
by Barnes & Noble, Inc., New York, N.Y. 10003
© J. G. Nichols 1969

Printed in Great Britain

Preface

I wish to thank Mr N.W. Bawcutt M.A. for help and criticism in the writing of the thesis which was the basis of this book.

All quotations from Jonson are from Herford and Simpson's *Ben Jonson*, which in the notes I refer to as Herford. Small capitals have not been retained in any quotations, and 's' has been modernized throughout.

Contents

Abbreviations used in the Footnotes

Castelain	M. Castelain. *Ben Jonson, L'Homme et l'Œuvre.* 1907.
Catullus	*Catullus, Tibullus, and Pervigilium Veneris*, Loeb edition. 1913.
Conversations	*Informations of Ben Johnston to W.D. when he came to Scotland upon foot 1619 Certain Informations and manners of Ben Johnsons to W. Drummond.*
Grierson	*The Poems of John Donne*, ed. H.J.C. Grierson. Volume I 1912, reprinted 1938.
Herford	*Ben Jonson*, ed. C.H. Herford and Percy Simpson (with, from 1938, Evelyn Simpson). 1925–52.
Smith	G. Gregory Smith. *Ben Jonson*. 1919.
Swinburne	A.C. Swinburne. *A Study of Ben Jonson*. 1889.
Symonds	J. Addington Symonds. *Ben Jonson*. 1886.
Walker	R.S. Walker. 'Ben Jonson's Lyric Poetry', *Seventeenth Century English Poetry*, ed. W.R. Keast. 1962.
Walton	Geoffrey Walton. 'The Tone of Ben Jonson's Poetry', *Metaphysical to Augustan. Studies in Tone and Sensibility in the Seventeenth Century*. 1955.
Trimpi	Wesley Trimpi. *Ben Jonson's Poems. A Study of the Plain Style*. 1962.
Tuve	Rosemond Tuve. *Elizabethan and Metaphysical Imagery*. 1947, Phoenix edition 1961.

C.P.	*Classical Philology.*
E.C.	*Essays in Criticism.*
E.L.H.	*English Literary History.*
J.E.G.P.	*Journal of English and Germanic Philology.*

ABBREVIATIONS USED IN THE FOOTNOTES

M.L.R.	*Modern Language Review.*
M.P.	*Modern Philology.*
P.C.	*Poetry (Chicago).*
P.M.L.A.	*Publications of the Modern Language Association.*
P.Q.	*Philological Quarterly.*
R.E.S.	*Review of English Studies.*
S.P.	*Studies in Philology.*
T.L.S.	*Times Literary Supplement.*

I

'A Big Fatt Man, that Spake
in Ryme'[1]

It may well seem that Jonson's position among the English poets is secure – foremost in the ranks of the great unread. His name (though, or because, naturally apt to be confused with that of Samuel Johnson) is well-known, his appearance even (grossly overweight, with a truculent expression on his pockmarked face) is not unfamiliar, and it is easy to remember him as the heavy writer of a few light lyrics. Some of these lyrics still find their way into anthologies and are generally popular; but by themselves they scarcely satisfy anyone worried by the thought that Jonson was, in his time, the most famous writer of his time, and the respected 'father' of a numerous offspring who also help to swell the pages of our anthologies. It is even more discomforting to think that the 'sons'' acceptance of Jonson's pre-eminence as poet is a critical estimate which their own poetic abilities should warn us against dismissing too easily. Of course, we must not exaggerate the respect given to Jonson in his own day: he was the target, though scarcely the victim, of many attacks; but they were the sort of attacks that witness to the fame and influence of the person attacked.

'Rare poemes', Jonson tells us, 'aske rare friends',[2] and certainly my impression is that friends of Jonson's poetry are nowadays scarce enough, whether or not they are 'rare' in that other sense of the word which mattered so much to Jonson. He was accustomed to hostility in his lifetime, and even seemed to court it and enjoy it; but it is not so much hostility as indifference that we are aware of when we open, for instance, a book with the title *Ben Jonson, A Collection of Critical Essays*[3] and find there not one essay devoted to the non-dramatic poems. This impression of neglect, a neglect not peculiar to our own century, is strengthened when we look at the selection of critical comments included in G.B. Johnston's edition of the poems,[4]

---

1. Francis Andrewes, 'Jonson's Visits to the Peak', Herford, XI, 388.
2. 'To Lvcy, Countesse of Bedford, with M^r. Donnes Satyres', Herford, VIII, 60.
3. Ed. Jonas A. Barish, 1963.
4. *Poems of Ben Jonson*, 1954, pp. xlix–liv.

comments ranging in time from Dryden to T. S. Eliot, and find they are concerned almost entirely with Jonson as a dramatist. It seems that Jonson was too sanguine when he mentioned in a letter of 1605 'posteritie that will hereafter read and Iudge my writings (though now neglected)'[1] and that Jonas A. Barish exaggerates only a little when he remarks that

> his poems remain unread even after the revolution in taste that has converted many of his metaphysical contemporaries into stars of the first magnitude.[2]

That some parts of even a great writer's work should be neglected need not, of course, surprise anyone – I doubt if *Titus Andronicus* has many admirers; but we should surely pause for thought when we remember that Jonson himself, who was an acute critic, certainly valued his poems above his plays. Even in 1616, with *Volpone* and *The Alchemist* behind him, he described his *Epigrammes* as 'the ripest of my studies'.[3] Unlike Shakespeare, he relied for his income as much on private patronage as on the public stage. While he always wrote non-dramatic verse, he forsook the theatre for long periods, and his returns to it seem sometimes due more to the failure of his other sources of income than to his natural inclination. *The New Inne*,[4] remembered now chiefly for the magnificent 'Ode *to himselfe*'[5] written after the play had been hissed and hooted off the boards, was produced after a ten years' absence from the theatre and was, hardly surprisingly, followed by another absence of three years. The poems themselves and the record of his talks with Drummond of Hawthornden show how he liked to think of himself, and liked others to think of him, primarily as a non-dramatic poet. Even in *Poetaster*,[6] performed during the 'War of the Theatres' when his ability as a playwright was under fire, he represented himself (or at least his ideals) on the stage in the character of Horace.[7]

---

1. Herford, I, 194.
2. Review of Trimpi, *M.P.*, LXI, No. 3 (February 1962), 240.
3. Dedication to *Epigrammes*, Herford, VIII, 25.
4. Herford, VI.
5. *Ibid.*, 492.
6. Herford, IV.
7. See J.B. Bamborough, *Ben Jonson*, 1959, p. 7; B.H. Newdigate, Preface, *The Poems of Ben Jonson*, 1936, pp. vii–viii. See Herford, I, 411–12, for the opinion that the character of Crites in *Cynthias Reuells* (Herford, IV) also bears a strong resemblance to Jonson himself.

If we think that the present neglect of the non-dramatic poems is not justified by their quality, we must account for it in other ways. To succeed in this would be to clear the ground for a better view of the essential qualities of Jonson's work; it might even lead us to suspect that the 'great lover and praiser of himself'[1] had good reason for his love and praise.

It has been suggested that Jonson is often 'punished for the crime of not being Shakespeare'.[2] For such a crime, who should 'scape whipping? Yet what Douglas Bush calls 'the conventional, not to say threadbare, contrast between Shakespeare and Jonson'[3] goes back a very long way:

> Through the whole of the seventeenth century Jonson's art and learning were contrasted with Shakespeare's natural gifts, as in Milton's verses in the Second Folio and in his tribute in *L'Allegro* to Shakespeare's 'native woodnotes wild'.[4]

Perhaps it is inevitable that contemporaries should be weighed against each other, even when one of them so obviously outweighs all others; yet, as though it were not inevitable, Jonson himself did his best to encourage it. There is his provocative remark to Drummond that 'Shakesperr wanted Arte',[5] and there are his comments on Shakespeare in *Discoveries* which are even more provocative because more considered:

> *I remember*, the Players have often mentioned it as an honour to Shakespeare, that in his writing, (whatsoever he penn'd) hee never blotted out line. My answer hath beene, Would he had blotted a thousand. Which they thought a malevolent speech.[6]

And not only the players, one is tempted to add. If we read on, however, we are bound to admit that this is not envy speaking, but friendship and admiration; the criticism may seem severe, but it is just:

> I had not told posterity this, but for their ignorance, who choose

1. *Conversations*, Herford, I, 151.
2. Jonas A. Barish, Intr. to *Ben Jonson, A Collection of Critical Essays*, p. 1.
3. *Classical Influences in Renaissance Literature*, 1952, p. 38.
4. Kenneth Muir, 'Changing Interpretations of Shakespeare', *A Guide to English Literature*, II, ed. Boris Ford, 1955, p. 286.
5. *Conversations*, Herford, I, 133.
6. Herford, VIII, 583.

that circumstance to commend their friend by, wherein he most faulted. And to justifie mine owne candor, (for I lov'd the man, and doe honour his memory (on this side Idolatry) as much as any.) . . . His wit was in his owne power; would the rule of it had beene so too.[1]

We see here that the contrast implied by Jonson between Shakespeare and himself can be a fruitful one. It suggests what we may hope to find in Jonson's poetry – conscious and scrupulous artistry, and also what we may hope to miss – casual and undisciplined writing. Of course we are reminded too of Shakespeare's unequalled fecundity and variety and, as Fuller's famous reminiscence makes plain, we must not expect these from Jonson:

> Many were the *wit-combats* betwixt him and *Ben Johnson*, which two I behold like a *Spanish great Gallion*, and an *English man of War*; Master *Johnson* (like the former) was built far higher in Learning; *Solid*, but *Slow* in his performances. *Shake-spear*, with the *English man of War*, lesser in *bulk*, but lighter in *sailing*, could turn with all tides, tack about and take advantage of all winds, by the quickness of his Wit and Invention.[2]

To make an obvious distinction, the wide variety of characters in Shakespeare's plays is not matched by Jonson. His scope is narrower, and the characters held up for admiration, in his plays and poems alike, tend to be idealized portraits of himself.[3] Even a description of Lucy, Countess of Bedford, calls Jonson himself to mind as forcibly as the Countess:

> *Onely a learned, and a manly soule*
> *I purpos'd her; that should, with euen powers,*
> *The rock, the spindle, and the sheeres controule*
> *Of destinie, and spin her owne free houres.*[4]

This contrast, then, seems to me not worth making if its purpose is to stress Shakespeare's superiority (that is too obvious), but useful if it reminds us that poets are not all of the same kind. The man who was 'built far higher in Learning' and '*Solid*, but *Slow*' may well have

---

1. Herford, VIII, 583–4.
2. *The History of the Worthies of England*, 1662, Herford, XI, 510.
3. See p. 2 above, and e.g. 'To the same', Herford, VIII, 55.
4. Herford, VIII, 52.

something of his own to offer, something we do not expect from Shakespeare.

Another comparison is frequently made, and one which in our day tends to be almost as damaging, though here we may be less ready to concede Jonson's inferiority. Again, it is a comparison that Jonson himself invites us to make, and again it is Drummond who records the invitation. Jonson told Drummond

> that Done for not keeping of accent deserved hanging[1]

and also

> that Done himself for not being ūnderstood would perish.[2]

My impression is that these remarks are much better known than Jonson's more appreciative comments on Donne. It is all too easy, I think, to take them as a declaration of war and then ally oneself automatically with Donne. Of course, even when Jonson described Donne to Drummond as 'the first poet jn the World' he added the characteristic qualification 'jn some things'.[3] As with Shakespeare, we have admiration tempered by stern criticism.

One illustration of the tendency to denigrate Jonson in comparison with Donne is the dispute over the famous four elegies whose authorship is doubtful. These are those printed as numbers XXXVIII, XXXIX, XL, and XLI in Jonson's *The Vnder-wood* in 1641.[4] Because this is a posthumous publication, because number XXXIX had been printed in the first edition of Donne's poems in 1633, and – most significant for my purpose – because all the poems are very good ones, some critics have doubted, or even denied, Jonson's authorship even of the three that are not found in Donne's works.

Castelain, arguing mainly from style, says that he thinks all four elegies are by Donne.[5] Herford and Simpson agree:

> One of them (XXXIX) appeared also among the elegies of Donne in 1633, and as all four are unmistakably by the same hand, and strangely recall Donne's strikingly individual manner, while they have no parallel in Jonson, his claim to them, published as they

---

1. *Conversations*, Herford, I, 133.
2. *Ibid.*, 138.
3. *Ibid.*, 135.
4. Herford, VIII, 191–9.
5. Castelain, p. 802 footnote.

were in the loose, ill-edited collection of the *Underwoods*, and after his death, cannot be asserted with any confidence, and must in our view be abandoned. Woman is, in both groups, the preoccupation of the writer. But to the author of the four 'elegies' woman is a daemonic power, exercising a mysterious spell which, with all his efforts at gaiety of heart, he never evades:

> *O, that you could but by dissection see*
> *How much you are the better part of me;*
> *How all my Fibres by your Spirit doe move,*
> *And that there is no life in me, but love.*
>
> *You would be then most confident, that tho*
> *Publike affaires command me now to goe*
> *Out of your eyes, and be awhile away;*
> *Absence, or Distance, shall not breed decay.*
>
> *Your forme shines here, here fixed in my heart:*
> *I may dilate my selfe, but not depart.*
>
> *Others by common Stars their courses run,*
> *When I see you, then doe I see my Sun,*
> *Till then 'tis all but darknesse, that I have;*
> *Rather then want your light, I wish a grave.*

Here surely we have a glimpse of the mystic passion, shot with splendour and gloom, which womanhood provoked in the genius of Donne. Jonson, whose highest mood towards women was an intellectual admiration, was impervious to this temper.[1]

However, George Williamson clearly does not regard Jonson as 'impervious to this temper', for he ascribes all four elegies to Jonson, suggesting that Jonson is here imitating Donne.[2] Evelyn Simpson's discussion is the most thorough and seems to me to come to the most reasonable conclusion. She ascribes 'The Expostulation' (the one which appears in both poets' works) to Donne, and the other three poems to Jonson.[3]

What we notice here, until we come to Evelyn Simpson's article, is a tendency to assume that Donne is a better poet than Jonson. There is really no other reason for ascribing to Donne the three elegies which

---

1. Herford, II, 384.
2. *The Donne Tradition*, 1930, pp. 191–3.
3. 'A Question of Authorship', *R.E.S.*, XV (1939), 274–82.

are nowhere published as his than the belief that they ar
Jonson's powers. Helen Gardner, in the introduction to he
edition of Donne's love-poems, does not attempt to ascril
three elegies to Donne. So far she agrees with Mrs Simpson;
latest twist in the story comes when, after agreeing that 'The Expostulation' cannot be by Jonson, she says:

It is the argument for Donne's authorship that needs scrutiny.[1]

Her scrutiny then leads her to deny Donne's authorship even of this
one![2]

Perhaps the attitude is changing.[3] Even as far back as 1933, R. S.
Walker – arguing for more appreciation of Jonson's lyric style – felt
it necessary to account for Donne's current popularity in terms that
suggested we should look for other qualities in Jonson.[4] More
recently, in 1961, John Hollander has pointed out that, if we compare
Jonson with Donne, we are likely to judge Jonson by standards which
are hardly relevant to his work.[5] Another recent apologist for Jonson's
poetry, Wesley Trimpi, also finds himself impelled to stress that
Donne does have his faults,[6] including those faults of roughness and
obscurity which Jonson pointed out to Drummond.[7] Trimpi's whole
book may be regarded as an attempt to find criteria suitable for
Jonson's work.

If the comparison with Donne is made, and I shall make it myself
from time to time, it is useful chiefly as a means of discriminating
between the two styles and isolating in either writer his distinctive-
ness. For the moment I shall merely suggest that Jonson's criticism of
Donne does (like his criticism of Shakespeare) have some justice in it,
and it does imply the standards which he set for his own work. He
disliked harsh rhythms, even if he did not always succeed in avoiding
them, and must have had little sympathy with Donne's boast:

---

1. *The Elegies and the Songs and Sonnets of John Donne*, 1965, p. xxxv.
2. *Ibid.*, p. xxxviii. M.L. Wilder's ascription of this poem to Jonson is unconvincing;
see 'Did Jonson write "The Expostulation" attributed to Donne?', *M.L.R.*, xxi (1926),
431–5.
3. G.A.E. Parfitt, 'The Poetry of Ben Jonson', *E.C.*, xviii, No. 1 (January 1968), 18–31,
agrees Jonson has been neglected and sees signs of a revival of interest.
4. Walker, p. 191.
5. Intr. to *Ben Jonson*, 1961, p. 10.
6. Trimpi, pp. 39–40.
7. *Conversations*, Herford, I, 133 and 138. Quoted above, p. 5.

*I sing not, Siren like, to tempt; for I
Am harsh ...*[1]

Similarly, the man who insisted that 'the chiefe vertue of a style is
perspicuitie'[2] must have thought that Donne, when he said that he
wrote his elegy on Prince Henry 'to match Sir Ed: Herbert jn
obscurenesse',[3] was making a joke in doubtful taste. At least, we
should not attribute Jonson's criticisms of Donne to mere spite or
envy: as with his comments on Shakespeare, there is more praise than
blame, and praise and blame together form a very illuminating critical
assessment.[4]

Sometimes it seems that Jonson himself is a bigger stumbling-
block to an appreciation of his own poetry than are any of his contemporaries. A. E. Housman, giving examples of what he considers to
be genuine poetry, says:

It is to be found again, Samuel, in your namesake, Benjamin, as
tough a piece of timber as yourself.[5]

'As tough a piece of timber as yourself'. It is remarkable how often
criticism of Jonson's poetry merges with criticism of Jonson the man,
and how often criticism of the man is adverse. I shall take one example
of this, a critic who dresses up in psychological jargon his dislike of
the man he thinks Jonson is. Edmund Wilson in his essay 'Morose
Ben Jonson', whose title loads the dice before the throwing starts,
suggests that Jonson exhibits all the symptoms of an 'anal-erotic' –
obstinacy, parsimony, and an obsession with order.[6] Furthermore:

Ben Jonson's enjoyment of tavern life and his great reputation for
wit have created, among those who do not read him, an entirely
erroneous impression of high spirits and joviality; but his portraits
show rather the face of a man who habitually worries, who is

---

1. 'To Mr *S.B.*', Grierson, p. 211.
2. *Discoveries*, Herford, VIII, 622.
3. The elegy is in Grierson, p. 267. Donne's comment was quoted by Jonson to Drummond, *Conversations*, Herford, I, 136.
4. See Walton, p. 27, note 6. For poems in praise of Donne, see Herford, VIII, 34, 60, 62.
5. *The Name and Nature of Poetry*, 1933, p. 31. I quote from the 1945 reprint. The
example Housman quotes from Jonson is '*An Elegie On the Lady* Jane Pawlet,
Marchion: of Winton', lines 1–4, Herford, VIII, 268.
6. *Ben Jonson, A Collection of Critical Essays*, ed. Jonas A. Barish, pp. 63–4. Wilson's
essay is from *The Triple Thinkers*, revised edition 1948 (first edition 1938).

sensitive and holds himself aloof, not yielding himself to intimate fellowship.[1]

This dubious estimate of Jonson's character, which leaves out of account his many and lasting friendships and the sheer *joie de vivre* evident in so much of his writing, leads on to a dubious estimate of his work:

> There is at times a peculiar coarseness in the texture of Jonson's writing, a strained falseness in his comic ideas, which, intolerable to a sober mind, may very well have seemed inspired to a constipated writer well primed with sack.[2]

One might develop this still further and suggest that Jonson wrote his poem 'On the Famovs Voyage'[3] as a compensation in fantasy for his own constipation; in which case posterity should be glad that Jonson was constipated, just as it should be glad that Maud Gonne refused to marry Yeats.[4] Speculation on these lines is, of course, endless – and futile. Perhaps Jonson was 'anal-erotic'; but if the symptoms of this neurosis are an obstinate dedication to the work in hand, the careful collecting of words, phrases, and ideas, and an obsessive urge to re-order the items in the collection, then probably all poets are 'anal-erotic' (for one might almost define poetry as highly-organized theft with a profitable redistribution of the stolen goods); and if all poets are 'anal-erotic', then the description will not serve to distinguish Jonson.

However, Jonson – who was not only truculent himself but also the cause that truculence is in other men – often seems to ask for this sort of treatment. Gifford, in the introduction to his edition, finds it necessary to defend Jonson against his detractors,[5] and Walker says plainly that the taste for biography is a hindrance to the enjoyment of Jonson as a poet, or at least as a lyric poet.[6]

---

1. *Ibid.*, p. 65.
2. *Ibid.*, p. 70.
3. Herford, VIII, 84.
4. She said to him, 'The world should thank me for not marrying you', Maud Gonne MacBride, *A Servant of the Queen*, 1938, p. 328. Quoted by A.N. Jeffares in *W.B. Yeats, Man and Poet*, 1949, p. 129.
5. William Gifford, 'Memoirs of Ben Jonson', *The Works of Ben Jonson*, I, ed. Francis Cunningham, p. vii and passim. Gifford's edition was first published in 1816.
6. Walker, p. 180.

Perhaps we should distinguish between the life and the work, as Herford and Simpson do when they say that 'Jonson exercised self-restraint in his art if not in his potations',[1] or as Inigo Jones, who had less cause than anyone to feel kindly towards Jonson, so charitably and intelligently does:

> *From henceforth this repute dwell with the ⟨e⟩ then,*
> *the best of Poettes but the worst of men.*[2]

On one occasion at least, Jonson asks that his personal failings should not be attributed to his 'Muse' whom he credits with just the opposite virtues:

> *So have you gain'd a Servant, and a Muse:*
> *The first of which, I feare, you will refuse;*
> *And you may justly, being a tardie, cold,*
> *Unprofitable Chattell, fat and old,*
> *Laden with Bellie, and doth hardly approach*
> *His friends, but to breake Chaires, or cracke a Coach.*
> *His weight is twenty Stone within two pound;*
> *And that's made up as doth the purse abound.*
> *Marrie the Muse is one, can tread the Aire,*
> *And stroke the water, nimble, chast, and faire,*
> *Sleepe in a Virgins bosome without feare,*
> *Run all the Rounds in a soft Ladyes eare,*
> *Widow or Wife, without the jealousie*
> *Of either Suitor, or a Servant by.*
> *Such, (if her manners like you) I doe send:*
> *And can for other Graces her commend,*
> *To make you merry on the Dressing stoole,*
> *A mornings, and at afternoones, to foole*
> *Away ill company, and helpe in rime*
> *Your Joane to passe her melancholie time.*
> *By this, although you fancie not the man,*
> *Accept his Muse . . .*[3]

We may say that Jonson's poetry is weighty, and we have his word for

---

1. Herford, I, 112.
2. 'To his false friend Mr. Ben Jonson', Herford, XI, 386.
3. '*Epistle. To my Lady* Covell', Herford, VIII, 230–1.

it that his body was, but we must not confuse two senses of the one word.

The distinction seems at first a valid one, and it is certainly better than Wilson's confusion, but in practice it is impossible to make, at least consistently. It may help us to appreciate some of the lyrics, but what are we to say of the rest of his non-dramatic work – epigrams on known people, epistles, complimentary poems, and even odes to himself? E. B. Partridge, objecting to Wilson's method, gives good reasons why we should not simply attack, or defend, or ignore Jonson the man:

> Surely there are better reasons for reading literature than to find out what Jonson or Shakespeare was really like. Yet such an answer does not meet Wilson's criticism on its own ground. As a matter of fact, we frequently do care what kind of man the author was, and our conception of him does play a part in the total response to his work. A better answer to Wilson, then, is this: his criticism may be right by chance, but his method is dubious, because he assumes that what a man writes in an artistic work completely and infallibly reveals his inner nature and that, from the distance of three hundred years, one can label a man by means of his diction. Both these assumptions seem to me wrong because they over-simplify the complex relations between art and character.[1]

The first of Jonson's *Epigrammes* forces the reader to come to terms with a powerful and self-assertive personality, and surely that is the merit of the poem:

> *Pray thee, take care, that tak'st my booke in hand,*
> *To reade it well: that is, to vnderstand.*[2]

We are the losers if we try to ignore the personality behind poems which are designed to reveal that personality:

> The difference between the plainness sought by the Royal Society and that of the classical plain style is that the former was a style in which the writer himself intruded as little as possible in the description of the physical world, a language as near to mathematics as possible. The classical plain style was developed to reveal

---

1. *The Broken Compass*, 1958, pp. 16–17.
2. 'To the Reader', Herford, VIII, 27.

the writer himself, to analyse and to portray the individual personality. The difference is not simply between philosophy and 'natural philosophy', but between the methods of analysis that each subject matter imposes. The conscious exclusion of the writer's personality – even his mind, if that were possible – in the language of mathematics is directly opposed to the cultivation of the individual and psychological search for philosophic truth.[1]

We surely miss most of the effect if we see in these lines from 'On my First Sonne' only a learned play on the derivation of the word '*poetrie*':

> Rest in soft peace, and, ask'd, say here doth lye
> Ben. Ionson his best piece of poetrie.[2]

The wit, the affection, and the pathos in those lines come partly from their being read in the context of all we know by Jonson and about him, from our knowledge that they were written by 'a great lover and praiser of himself, a contemner and Scorner of others'[3] who said bluntly that his *Epigrammes* were '*no ill pieces*'.[4]

It is difficult to know how best to reply to those who 'fancie not the man';[5] but at least I would suggest that it is a witness to the quality of the poems that the personality comes through. Moreover, Jonson often shows more self-knowledge than he is given credit for, and a disarming ability to laugh at his own foibles which makes even his self-assertion more palatable. When Drummond tells us that Jonson is 'given rather to losse a friend, than a Jest',[6] we may be inclined to nod our heads in sympathy with Drummond and applaud his insight; but it is worth remembering that Jonson had already applied this proverbial expression[7] to himself in *Poetaster* where Tucca describes Horace, alias Jonson, in this way:

. . . hee will pen all hee knowes. A sharpe thornie-tooth'd *satyricall* rascall, flie him; hee carries hey in his horne: he wil sooner lose his best friend, then his least iest.[8]

---

1. Trimpi, p. 91.
2. Herford, VIII, 41.
3. *Conversations*, Herford, I, 151.
4. Dedication, *Epigrammes*, Herford, VIII, 26.
5. Herford, VIII, 231. Quoted above, p. 10.
6. *Conversations*, Herford, I, 151.
7. M.P. Tilley, *A Dictionary of the Proverbs in England in the Sixteenth and Seventeenth Centuries*, 1950, p. 244.
8. IV. iii. 108–11, Herford, IV, 269.

Perhaps Drummond suffered from constipation too?
Herford and Simpson are surely right when they say:

> . . . his work is, in a rare degree, of a piece; we can distinguish its phases and its kinds; but the note of Jonsonian personality is singularly continuous; the apprentice challenging the veterans of Spain and the old poet inditing an Ode to Himself are the same . . .[1]

Nevertheless, we must also expect some variety of attitude, and not be amazed if Jonson shows different moods in different poems.[2] Herford and Simpson seem to be shocked to find this variety in *Epigrammes:*

> In this very collection, only a couple of pages from the beautiful morning hymn to the Countess of Bedford, the reader comes upon an epigram which suggests in the plainest terms that all women are harlots.[3]

We must always allow for hyperbole, and it is a pity when we let even our chivalry come between us and a good poem, as I think Jonson's editors do again here:

> What Jonson's special quarrel with Cecily Bulstrode was, we do not know. Certainly few men in his day, or in any day, have assailed a woman with the foul-mouthed ferocity of his lines to 'The Court Pucell' (*Underwoods*, xlix). The erotic verses addressed to her by one of her intimates (probably either Donne or Roe)[2] [in footnote '2 See *The Poems of John Donne*, ed. Grierson, i. 410'] sufficiently attest her character. But Jonson impatiently flings aside the dignity of just rebuke (which indeed he had little title to administer), in order to outdo her in ribald abuse. It is not Juvenal denouncing Messalina, or Knox rebuking Mary, that the spectacle recalls, but Pope hitching into rhyme his acrid and shameless gibes at Lady Mary Wortley Montagu.[4]

This comment misses the tone of the poem, which is established in the first two lines:

---

1. Herford, I, 120.
2. See below, p.64, note 1.
3. Herford, II, 367.
4. Herford, I, 59.

Do's the Court-Pucell then so censure me,
And thinkes I dare not her? let the world see.[1]

Jonson is not merely letting rip with 'foul-mouthed ferocity'. He shows he is conscious of what he is doing, and 'let the world see' is an invitation to us to judge how far he is capable of maintaining the attack. I do not suggest that this poem has the wit of Donne, but it is similar to Donne's elegies in that much of the reader's interest comes from seeing how many variations can be played on one apparently simple theme. Then there is the terse and sensuous force of 'lip-thirstie' and the moral weight in:

And as lip-thirstie, in each words expence,
Doth labour with the Phrase more then the sense?

Jonson had no patience with those who enjoyed the mere sound of words so much that they neglected, in their concentration on the manner of expression, to pay attention to the matter.[2] The energetic close of the poem is particularly striking:

The wits will leave you, if they once perceive
You cling to Lords, and Lords, if them you leave
For Sermoneeres: of which now one, now other,
They say you weekly invite with fits o' th' Mother,
And practise for a Miracle; take heed
*   This Age would lend no faith to* Dorrels *Deed:*
Or if it would, the Court is the worst place,
*   Both for the Mothers, and the Babes of grace,*
For there the wicked in the Chaire of scorne,
*   Will cal't a Bastard, when a Prophet's borne.*

The pun in 'fits o'th' Mother' brings together, just at the right moment, the themes of hysteria and sexual indulgence. The mock-solemn warning

take heed
This Age would lend no faith to Dorrels *Deed*[3]

---

1. Herford, VIII, 222.
2. Discussed in more detail below, pp. 74–5.
3. John Darrel, Puritan preacher and religious charlatan. See Herford, x, 251. Cf. *Conversations*, Herford, I, 146: 'a Gentlewoman fell jn such a Phantasie or Phrensie wt one Mr Dod a Puritan preacher yt she requested her husband that for the procreation of ane Angel or Saint he might lye wt her, which having obtained it was bot ane ordinarie birth'.

leads neatly to the crushing Drydenesque blow at the end:

> *For there the wicked in the Chaire of scorne,*
> *Will cal't a Bastard, when a Prophet's borne.*

With the allusion to Psalm I[1] in 'the wicked in the Chaire of scorne' the poem goes beyond the 'Court-Pucell' to include the 'Sermoneeres'[2] in an attack which parodies their own way of speaking. I think there is more subtlety in this poem than Herford and Simpson allow for, and I think it is their preoccupation with the personalities involved that prevents their seeing this poem as valuable to us now primarily as a work of art.

Perhaps there is no middle position, and we must be either attracted or repelled by Jonson's character. Yet I shall suggest a point of view from which even Jonson's boasting, and that even when it is without self-mockery, may be looked at with pleasure. Jonson is the hero of a legend, an epic legend which he did more than anyone else to create, and we must always be prepared for an epic hero to boast. We take it from Beowulf:

> ... the best and wisest among my countrymen urged me to visit you, King Hrothgar, because they knew of my vast strength. They were eye-witnesses of it when, stained with the blood of my adversaries, I emerged from a fight in which I destroyed an entire family of giants – capturing five of them – besides killing, by night, a number of sea-monsters. Although hard pressed, I destroyed the brutes (who had courted trouble) and avenged their attacks upon the Geats. And now I mean to deal single-handed with the monstrous Grendel.[3]

We take it from Odysseus:

> ... there is no one I'm too proud to take on; in fact I'm ready to meet and match myself against all comers. For I am not a bad hand all round at any kind of manly sport.[4]

---

1. Verse I.
2. 'The only example in the *O.E.D.*; a contemptuous variant of "sermoner"', Herford, XI, 88.
3. *Beowulf*, trans. David Wright, 1957, p. 36.
4. *The Odyssey*, trans. E. V. Rieu, 1946 (quotation from reprint 1964), p. 127.

We may also take it from Jonson, and for the same reason – that it is nobly expressed:

> *Wee'l rip our Richest veynes*
> *And once more stryke the eare of tyme wth those ffresh straynes:*
> *As shall besides delyght*
> *And Cunninge of their grownde*
> *Give cause to some of wonnder, some despite,*
> *But vnto more dispayre to Imitate their sounde.*[1]

A boast is still more acceptable when we cannot deny its truth, and Jonson did not exaggerate even a little when he boasted that

> he was better Versed & knew more jn Greek and Latin, than all the Poets jn England...[2]

But, although no one denies his great learning, time and again we meet the suggestion, or implication, that the learning smothered the poetry. Gilbert Highet, making the routine contrast, mentions

> Shakespeare's liking for the classics, his sensitive ear, his retentive memory, and the transforming magic of his eloquence[3]

and then says curtly:

> Others, like Jonson, stud their pages with quotation-marks, and talk in italics.[3]

J. A. Symonds puts the objection even more strongly:

> Like many poets whom the muses love, Jonson uttered his best things by accident, and what weighed heavily upon his genius was the fixed idea that scholarship and sturdy labour could supply the place of inspiration.[4]

Of course 'scholarship and sturdy labour' cannot 'supply the place of inspiration' (whatever that may be), but I know of no evidence that Jonson thought they could, and I think it is reckless to assume that they are likely to hinder the creative act. Milton and Samuel Johnson

---

1. *'Ode:'*, Herford, VIII, 420.
2. *Conversations*, Herford, I, 149.
3. *The Classical Tradition. Greek and Roman Influences on Western Literature*, 1949 (quotations from corrected edition 1951), p. 218.
4. Symonds, p. 63. Symonds is speaking of Jonson's translations.

spring to mind as poets who were also scholars, as men whose poetry is hardly imaginable without their scholarship; and is there one English poet who did not use any of his reading in his poetry? However, there is a difference between being well-read and being a scholar and, as Symonds implies, a poet may often use his reading in an unscholarly and accidental way. Jonson was a scholar and, when he borrowed from other writers, was usually aware that he was doing so, indeed capable even of supplying chapter and verse for his sources when necessary.[1] But, although to be a scholar may be less than to be a poet, ought we to object if a man can be both at once?

Unfortunately, an awareness of Jonson's learning can lead to a more subtle and radical objection. Castelain, speaking of the poems to Charis,[2] expresses an unease which many people must feel when reading Jonson:

Malheureusement ils ne sont pas très personnels. Sans doute, tous les poèmes de ce genre sont, pour le fond au moins, voués à la banalité; le cercle des idées est forcément restreint. Depuis tant d'années qu'il y a des hommes, et qui aiment, ou du moins qui sont amoureux, on s'est probablement avisé de toutes les façons qu'il y a dans toutes les langues de dire à une femme qu'elle est adorable. Par conséquent, la forme, le détail est tout; mais l'ennui avec Jonson, c'est qu'on ne sait jamais, en l'admirant, si l'on n'est pas la dupe d'une fraude innocente ou plutôt de sa propre ignorance. Les trois premières pièces au moins et l'entretien avec Cupidon rappellent beaucoup, pour l'idée générale et même dans les détails du style, certains morceaux de l'Anthologie. Et si les autres semblent plus originales, qui nous dit que certains vers charmants ne viennent pas en droite ligne de Catulle ou d'Anacréon, que tel passage admiré par nous n'est pas une simple traduction bien faite ou une ingénieuse adaptation?[3]

(Unfortunately, they are not very individual. Doubtless all poems of this kind are bound to be commonplace, at least basically; the range of ideas is necessarily limited. During the many years that

---

1. As he did, at Prince Henry's request, for *The Masqve of Qveenes*; see Herford, VII, 281. Some idea of how much Jonson borrowed may be gained from W.D. Briggs, 'Source-Material for Jonson's "Epigrams" and "Forest"', *C.P.*, XI (January–October 1916), 169–90.

2. 'A Celebration of Charis in ten Lyrick Peeces', Herford, VIII, 131–42.

3. Castelain, p. 838.

men have existed, and been in love or at least felt amorous, every possible way in every language of telling a woman that she is adorable has probably been thought of. Consequently, the form and the detail are everything; but the trouble with Jonson is that you never know, when you are admiring him, whether or not you are the victim of an innocent deception or rather of your own ignorance. The first three pieces at least, and the discourse with Cupid, strongly recall, in their general conception and even in stylistic details, certain passages from the Greek Anthology. And if the others seem more original, who can assure us that certain charming lines do not come directly from Catullus or from Anacreon, that the passage we admire is not simply a neat translation or an ingenious adaptation?)

A quick retort to Castelain might mention many another 'ingénieuse adaptation' and ask if he objected to, say, Shakespeare's adapting Plutarch; but this would not really meet his objection, which is mainly that Jonson does not use his sources creatively, that he lacks originality, and that only the reader's 'propre ignorance' prevents his recognizing 'une simple traduction bien faite' for what it is. We have an advantage over Castelain in that we can now supplement our own ignorance by reference to Herford and Simpson's learned commentary on the poems; and yet the doubt remains. Did Jonson lack originality?

Ignoring for the moment the 'ingénieuse adaptation', I do not think that even 'une simple traduction bien faite' is really so simple. Certainly Castelain's own example does not help his case, for he chooses the justly famous 'Drinke to me, onely, with thine eyes':[1]

Vous vous récriez: c'est une petite merveille, un bijou! il n'y a rien de plus gracieux dans toute la poésie contemporaine! Et voilà qu'un jour, par hasard, on découvre les quatre petites phrases, qui forment cette bluette exquise, dans quatre lettres de Philostrate. Elles se retrouvent là à peu près mot pour mot: Jonson s'est seulement donné la peine de les traduire et de les mettre bout à bout. Et sans doute la traduction est très bien faite et la musique en est exquise; mais cela n'enlève-t-il pas aussi beaucoup de son mérite?[2]

(You exclaim, 'It is a little miracle, a jewel! There is nothing more

---

1. Herford, VIII, 106.
2. Castelain, p. 840.

graceful in the whole of contemporary poetry!' And then there comes the day when, by chance, you discover the four little phrases, which go to make up this exquisite trifle, in four epistles of Philostratus. They are to be found there almost word for word: Jonson has merely taken the trouble to translate them and to place them end to end. The translation is certainly very well done and it is exquisitely musical; but does not that also take away much of its merit?)

Foreign literatures are full of phrases waiting to be translated almost word for word and placed end to end. Surely anyone who can select the right ones, and translate and combine them as felicitously as Jonson does here, is a poet? There are many ways in which a poet can work, and this way seems to me as valid as any other. John Palmer shows more insight than Castelain into the paradoxical nature of translation when he says of this poem:

> Here is crowning proof that Jonson was never more natural than when he uttered himself in quotations.[1]

Palmer's comment implies also that we oversimplify the issue if we argue, as Hugh Kenner does, that Jonson does not want us to enjoy any classical echoes in this poem:

> So completely does the poem inhabit the English idiom that no one is likely to think of hunting for sources.[2]

The trouble is that many people do 'think of hunting for sources', and in 1815 Dovaston found the sources of the poem we are discussing.[3] Kenner argues that, if it took two hundred years for the sources to be discovered, then Jonson did not expect the reader to be aware of them.[4] I find it difficult to imagine a Jonson so lenient to his readers' ignorance. I think we gain an extra pleasure if we know something of the genesis of the poem, and I think that Jonson meant that we should. Castelain wants 'originality', and Hugh Kenner seems to want at least the illusion of it. What did Jonson and his contemporaries want?

---

1. *Ben Jonson*, 1934, p. 298.
2. Intr. to *Seventeenth Century Poetry, The Schools of Donne and Jonson*, 1964, p. xxvi.
3. John F.M. Dovaston, Letter to *The Monthly Magazine*, XXXIX (March 1815), 123–4. This letter is mentioned, and the source-passages from the *Epistles* of Philostratus are quoted, in Herford, XI, 39. The first time the sources were noted in print seems to have been in 1785; see A.D. Fitton Brown, 'Drink to me, Celia', *M.L.R.*, LIV (1959), 555, footnote 1.
4. *Loc. cit.*

Originality and novelty are recent virtues, and the Renaissance did not demand of 'making' or 'feigning' as poetry was frequently called in English, that it work out of whole cloth.[1]

What the Renaissance did demand was that the finished poem, whatever its origins, should be a unified piece of work. Jonson denied that his poems were merely made up of 'common places filch'd'[2]. In his attack on 'Poore Poet-Ape' he stresses that it is the wholeness of the end-result that matters:

> *Foole, as if halfe eyes will not know a fleece*
> *From locks of wooll, or shreds from the whole peece?*[3]

Jonson's contemporaries knew as well as we do that his poetry was deeply indebted to his reading, but they were not so ready as we may sometimes be to regard this as a fault. It is true that Inigo Jones mocked:

> *the good's translation, butt the ill's thyne owne*[4]

but contemporaries were more likely to emphasize the change that Jonson effected:

> *... whatsoere was strange*
> *Or borrow'd in thee did grow thine by th' change.*[5]

Nor was Drummond complaining when he said:

> his jnventions are smooth and easie, but above all he excelleth jn a translation.[6]

At that time it was a recognized practice for poets to draw on other poets for their materials, and particularly on what has been called 'the traditional and international gold reserve'.[7] This is, indeed, still the practice among poets; but it is no longer such a respectable thing to do, or to be found out doing.

Bearing in mind the warning that 'we must not think of Jonson's

---

1. John Hollander, *op. cit.*, p. 23.
2. '*Epistle* To Elizabeth Covntesse of Rvtland', Herford, VIII, 116.
3. *Ibid.*, 45.
4. 'To his false friend M.' Ben Iohnson', Herford, XI, 385.
5. I. Mayne, '*To the Memory of* Ben. Ionson', *ibid.*, 454.
6. *Conversations*, Herford, I, 151.
7. Douglas Bush, *op. cit.*, p. 23. See also Hardin Craig, *The Enchanted Glass, The Elizabethan Mind in Literature*, 1936, pp. 254–5.

humanism as nourished in the leisured and fastidious seclusion of
Horton',[1] we should now find it fruitful to look in more detail at
Jonson's attitude to the classics and examine the results of this
attitude in some of the poems. For a start, Jonson's respect for the
ancients is far from idolatry:

> It is true they open'd the gates, and made the way, that went before
> us; but as Guides, not Commanders...[2]

Later in *Discoveries* he expands on this:

> The third requisite in our *Poet*, or Maker, is *Imitation*, to bee able
> to convert the substance, or Riches of an other *Poet*, to his owne
> use. To make choise of one excellent man above the rest, and so to
> follow him, till he grow very Hee: or, so like him, as the Copie may
> be mistaken for the Principall. Not, as a Creature, that swallowes,
> what it takes in, crude, raw, or indigested; but, that feedes with an
> Appetite, and hath a Stomacke to concoct, divide, and turne all
> into nourishment . . . But, that, which wee especially require in
> him is an exactness of Studie, not alone enabling him to know the
> *History*, or Argument of a *Poeme*, and to report it: but so to master
> the matter, and Stile, as to shew, hee knowes, how to handle, place,
> or dispose of either, with *elegancie*, when need shall bee.[3]

This theory is much more subtle than a 'fixed idea that scholarship
and sturdy labour could supply the place of inspiration',[4] and what
follows makes an interesting comment on the view of poets that sees
them producing their 'best things by accident':[5]

> And not thinke, hee can leape forth suddainely a *Poet*, by dreaming
> hee hath been in *Parnassus*, or, having washt his lipps (as they say)
> in *Helicon*. There goes more to his making, then so. For to Nature,
> Exercise, Imitation, and Studie, *Art* must bee added, to make all
> these perfect.[6]

That, in brief, is Jonson's theory, as far removed from slavish
adherence to models and mere theft of other men's achievements as it

1. Herford, I, 8.
2. *Discoveries*, Herford, VIII, 567.
3. *Ibid.*, 638–9.
4. Symonds, p. 63. Quoted above, p. 16.
5. *Ibid.*
6. *Discoveries*, Herford, VIII, 639.

is from any idea of poets as the Lucky Jims of the literary world. It is a high ideal, and of course Jonson did not always live up to it. Herford and Simpson make an interesting distinction:

> ... Jonson has given us a clue to the conditions of his real power even as a translator. When he is not trying to render completely, but is seeking, on his own terms, to choose and leave, refashion and recombine, Jonson is one of the great masters of this art in our literature. 'Drinke to me, onely, with thine eyes' more than atones for the *De Arte Poetica*. It would seem as if the semi-servile labour of fitting his mind implicitly to another's actually inhibited half its force; while the more inspiring call to educe the hidden, and collect the scattered, and exalt and glorify the inchoate and inexpressive, put him upon his mettle, and brought the energies of his intellect into full play.[1]

There is much truth here, but we can even see Jonson transform his models when they are poetic masterpieces, far from 'inchoate and inexpressive'; this transformation can take place even when he makes 'une ingénieuse adaptation'[2] of Catullus.

Jonson's '*Song*. To Celia'[3] is in part an adaptation of Catullus's 'Vivamus, mea Lesbia, atque amemus'.[4] The poem that follows it in *The Forrest*, 'To the same',[5] is adapted from both 'Vivamus, mea Lesbia, atque amemus' and 'Qvaeris, quot mihi basiationes'.[6] Herford and Simpson comment:

> When ... Jonson tried the capacity of his English upon a great poet like Catullus, he rarely achieves more than mediocrity. The simple intensity of
>
> *Soles occidere et redire possunt:*
> *Nobis, cum semel occidit brevis lux,*
> *Nox est perpetua una dormienda*
>
> offered no vantage ground for the salient qualities of Jonson's style, and became, 'literally' rendered, merely smooth and insignificant in his

---

1. Herford, II, 409.
2. Castelain, p. 838. Quoted above, p. 17.
3. Herford, VIII, 102.
4. Catullus, No. V, pp. 6–8.
5. Herford, VIII, 103.
6. Catullus, No. VII, pp. 8–10.

Sunnes, that set, may rise againe:
But if once we loose this light,
'Tis, with vs, perpetuall night.[1]

I agree that Jonson's poems are inferior to Catullus's; but, while admitting that Jonson has lost a quality we admire in Catullus, we may see also that his poems have other qualities not found in the Catullus. As Douglas Bush says, 'in the songs derived from Catullus ... there is more courtliness than passion, and no hint of the metaphysical fourth dimension';[2] but, as Bush says elsewhere:

As soon as we begin Jonson's

Come, my Celia, let us prove,
While we may, the sports of love,

we know that we are intended to enjoy a light adaptation of Catullus, a picture of the sophisticated game of love as played in ancient Rome or modern London ... these obvious remarks are by way of distinction, not disparagement of the lesser poet. Jonson was much too fine an artist, and much too tough-minded an observer of life, to reveal more than traces of the pedantry of neoclassicism.[3]

If we must not expect an exact reproduction of the sense or tone of Catullus, neither must we expect an attempt to write English as though it were Latin:

Jonson made no attempt to impose the idiom and syntax of the classical writers on the English language. The spirit in which he uses the classics is very different from that of Milton.[4]

Hugh Kenner goes into more detail on this point; after comparing

All the grasse that Rumney *yeelds,*
Or the sands in Chelsey *fields,*
Or the drops in siluer Thames,
Or the starres, that guild his streames,
In the silent sommer-nights,

---

1. Herford, II, 386. The sense of the Latin is: Suns may set and rise again: for us, when once our brief light has died, there is one uninterrupted night for sleeping.
2. *English Literature in the Earlier Seventeenth Century 1600–1660*, 1945, p. 106.
3. *Classical Influences in Renaissance Literature*, p. 39.
4. F.W. Bradbrook, 'Ben Jonson's Poetry', *A Guide to English Literature*, III, ed. Boris Ford, 1956, p. 134.

with

When youths ply their stolne delights[1]

quam magnus numerus Libyssae harenae
lasarpiciferis iacet Cyrenis,
oraclum Iovis inter aestuosi
et Batti veteris sacrum sepulcrum,
aut quam sidera multa, cum tacet nox,
furtivos hominum vident amores[2]

(As great as the number of the Libyan sands that lie in silphium-bearing Cyrene, between the oracle of fiery Jove and the sacred tomb of ancient Battus, or as many as the stars which, when night is silent, see the stealthy loves of men ...)

he says:

English does not lend itself to an encircling syntax, pausing on the numerous stars to make them look down on furtive lovers; its genius, Jonson senses, is to press forward. In a time heavy with reforming pedantries, when inevitably by one means or another English and Latin poetry were going to be brought to some common rule, it was Jonson alone who saw how to align the vernacular's energies with the best of what learned men knew.[3]

We may notice too that Jonson replaces Catullus's contemporary references by contemporary references of his own. Jonson is making something that can live in his world; he is not trying to polish a museum-piece.

It is not helpful, however, to distinguish Jonson from Catullus merely in order to align him with a poet with whom he has probably less in common. This is what F. W. Bradbrook does when he says:

Jonson's ... poem to Celia ('Kiss me sweet') ... perfectly catches the tone and accent of its original in the opening lines. Then, in the enumeration of the kisses, the lyric deviates ironically, and contrasts Catullus with the Cockney background of the contemporary lover ... In the last four lines of the lyric Jonson returns to the urbane and poised accent of the opening. Such flexible and controlled transitions from an ideal classical world to the actualities of

---

1. 'To the same', Herford, VIII, 103.
2. Catullus, No. VII, pp. 8–10.
3. Kenner, *op. cit.*, p. xxvii.

seventeeth-century London, with the accompanying sense of ironic contrast ...[1]

No, it will not do merely to assimilate Jonson into a taste for T. S. Eliot.[2]

> *Kisse me, sweet: The warie louer*
> *Can your fauours keepe, and couer,*
> *When the common courting iay*
> *All your bounties will betray*[3]

is very different from:

> *Vivamus, mea Lesbia, atque amemus,*
> *rumoresque senum severiorum*
> *omnes unius aestimemus assis.*[4]

(Let us live, my Lesbia, and let us love, and let us value at a farthing all the murmurs of stern old men.)

The contrast in Jonson is not between the amorous young and the stern old, but between courtly and less courtly lovers. He is commenting on manners, on the secrecy which convention demanded of a lover, and his tone is appropriately lighter than Catullus's. Then there is nothing 'Cockney' about the contemporary setting which Jonson gives to his poem. Moreover, to see a contrast between 'an ideal classical world' and 'the actualities of seventeenth-century London' is to ignore the attractiveness of Jonson's picture of London here and scarcely to have read Catullus at all.

The whole of 'Come my Celia'[5] and the last four lines of 'Kisse me, sweet'[6] were included in *Volpone*,[7] and the fact that they are songs originally used in a comedy suggests some of the qualities we should look for in them. Both poems are lighter than Catullus's, concerned with 'the sports of loue'[8] rather than an obsessive passion, and with love in a social setting rather than *l'égoisme à deux*. To the first poem

---

1. Bradbrook, *op. cit.*, pp. 135–6.
2. As F.W. Bradbrook does, *op. cit.*, p. 136.
3. 'To the same', Herford, VIII, 103.
4. Catullus, No. V, p. 6.
5. Herford, VIII, 102.
6. *Ibid.*, 103.
7. III. vii. 165–83 and 236–9, Herford, V, 82 and 84.
8. '*Song*. To Celia', Herford, VIII, 102.

Jonson adds, with a Latinate pun on the meaning of 'rumour' which *fama* can have (an instance of learning borne with a witty grace), an acknowledgement of the effect which the affair can have on the lovers' reputations:

> *Why should we deferre our ioyes?*
> *Fame, and rumor are but toyes.*[1]

Then Jonson's jealous third party, in contrast with the 'malus'[2] of Catullus, is not expected to use witchcraft against the lovers:

> *Cannot we delude the eyes*
> *Of a few poore houshold spyes?*
> *Or his easier eares beguile,*
> *So remoued by our wile?*[3]

When Jonson recommends secrecy in love, as he does also in his second poem, it is in accordance with a social and literary convention, and not to avoid witchcraft:

> *'Tis no sinne, loues fruit to steale,*
> *But the sweet theft to reueale:*
> *To be taken, to be seene,*
> *These haue crimes accounted beene.*[4]

Here also the contrasts between sin and crime, and between what is and what is only 'accounted' to be something, show an urbanity which is not in the Catullus and is not intended to be. The end of Jonson's second poem:

> *That the curious may not know*
> *How to tell' hem, as th⟨e⟩y flow,*
> *And the eniuous, when they find*
> *What their number is, be pin'd.*[5]

is concerned obviously with curiosity and envy, but not in the same way as Catullus is. Jonson sees them merely as social discomforts which it would be more pleasant to avoid, but Catullus is referring to the superstition that it was bad luck to number one's blessings, and

1. *Ibid.*
2. Catullus, No. v, p. 8.
3. '*Song*. To Celia', Herford, VIII, 102.
4. *Ibid.*
5. 'To the same', *ibid.*, 103.

he shows too, in his use of 'invidere', that he is afraid of an evil spell being cast upon the lovers:

> *dein, cum milia multa fecerimus,*
> *conturbabimus illa, ne sciamus,*
> *aut nequis malus invidere possit,*
> *cum tantum sciat esse basiorum.*[1]

(Then, when we have accumulated many thousands [of kisses], we shall confuse our counting, so that we may not know the number, and so that no wicked person may put the evil eye upon them when he knows how very many kisses there are.)

In 'Qvaeris, quot mihi basiationes' too Catullus is afraid that the lovers may be bewitched:

> *tam te basia multa basiare*
> *vesano satis et super Catullost,*
> *quae nec pernumerare curiosi*
> *possint nec mala fascinare lingua.*[2]

(To kiss you with so many kisses is enough and more than enough for mad Catullus, kisses not to be counted by the inquisitive nor bewitched by an evil tongue.)

Jonson's poems, then, are slight and sprightly, while Catullus's are more than a little sad. There is nothing in Jonson with the plangency of

> *nox est perpetua una dormienda*[3]

(There is one uninterrupted night for sleeping)

and nothing so magnificent, but anything in the tone of that line would have been out of place in the lyrics he was writing.

Laurence Lerner defines very well the sort of enjoyment we can get from poems like these if we know their origins, while emphasizing that we can still enjoy them if we have never heard of Catullus:

At the height of his seduction scene, Volpone sings to Celia a version of one of Catullus's most famous poems. As well as the

---

1. Catullus, No. v, p. 8.
2. *Ibid.*, No. vii, p. 10.
3. *Ibid.*, No. v, p. 6.

beauty of Jonson's lyric, as well as its dramatic appropriateness, the fact that it is Catullus also matters. The *imitatio* is a tribute to the original; a reminder, satisfying to the audience, of its continuing power. This *imitatio*, this reminder, is a literary merit in itself. If we complain ... that this is to restrict poetry to an educated elite, there are two answers. One is that this is strictly a social rather than a literary complaint, like complaining that a book is published only in a limited and expensive edition: if the groundlings had known Latin, the complaint would vanish. And secondly, this is after all only a minor aim in *Volpone*, a sort of extra: the main literary effect of the poem is quite independent of knowing that it is from Catullus....[1]

F. R. Leavis stresses the moral implications of *imitatio*, which he regards not as something which affords us an 'ironic contrast' between a glorious past and a sordid present, but as a means of entering 'into an ideal community' affected by 'contemporary life and manners' and itself affecting them:

> Jonson's effort was to feel Catullus, and the others he cultivated, as contemporary with himself; or rather, to achieve an English mode that should express a sense of contemporaneity with them. The sense itself, of course, had to be achieved by effort, and was achieved in the mode. This mode, which is sufficiently realized in a considerable body of poems, may be described as consciously urbane, mature, and civilized. Whatever its relation to any Latin originals, it is indisputably *there*, an achieved actuality. It belongs, of course, to literature, and is the product of a highly refined sensibility; yet it is at the same time expressive, if to a large degree by aspiration only, of a way of living. In it the English poet, who remains not the less English and of his own time, enters into an ideal community, conceived of as something with which contemporary life and manners may and should have close relations.[2]

This is similar to H. A. Mason's conception of the proper use of the classics:

> Jonson, I believe, and no other Englishman before him, gives us

---

1. *The Truest Poetry. An Essay on the Question, What is Literature?*, 1960, p. 116.
2. *Revaluation*, 1936, p. 19.

the answer. The Classics are properly used when they enable an Englishman to become fully aware, that is, in his own idiom, of the aspirations to conceive life in ideal terms which are found in all attempts to make life civilized. This answer enables us to distinguish the mere Humanist, who, as it were, has the Classics in his head, from the true Humanist who has *translated* the Classics into the only form in which they can still live.[1]

Perhaps that is what Jonson had in mind when, after saying that

he was better Versed & knew more jn Greek and Latin, than all the Poets jn England

he added cryptically:

and quintessence ⟨th⟩ their braines.[2]

A modern reader may, however, still feel uneasy before these adaptations of Catullus. Even if he concedes 'originality' of a sort, he is likely to ask 'How deeply were these poems felt?' or 'What happens to the poet's sincerity under this weight of careful and conscious adaptation?'

One characteristic of Jonson's variety is that he often treated a poetic convention seriously in one work and satirized or burlesqued it in another. It is, of course, possible to enjoy both the serious treatment and the burlesque; and it is not a necessary part of the enjoyment to struggle with the question of which treatment mirrors the poet's heart most clearly.[3]

It is significant that Johnston thought he had to mention, even if only to dismiss, 'the question of which treatment mirrors the poet's heart most clearly'. Poems are often studied as autobiographical sketches or, more subtly, as psychological documents. They may be always both these things but, if they are, it is frequently in a way very different from an obvious, easily-interpreted statement of the poet's feelings. Even when a poem can be interpreted in this fashion, even when it

---

1. *Humanism and Poetry in the Early Tudor Period*, 1959, p. 289. Compare John Hollander, *op. cit.*, p. 24: 'His "translations" proper never aim at preserving a particular poem...but at carrying over a method, a style, a way of writing, thought and life.'
2. *Conversations*, Herford, I, 149.
3. G.B. Johnston, Intr. to *Poems of Ben Jonson*, p. xxxvii.

seems to ask to be interpreted in this fashion, it is also something much more important than a set of psychological data:

> *Vague as fog and looked for like mail.*
> *Farther off than Australia.*
> *Bent-backed Atlas, our travelled prawn.*
> *Snug as a bug and at home*
> *Like a sprat in a pickle jug.*
> *A creel of eels, all ripples.*
> *Jumpy as a Mexican bean.*
> *Right, like a well-done sum.*
> *A clean slate, with your own face on.*[1]

I quote this mainly because it is so different from anything by Jonson. There are strong feelings here and, since the feelings and sensations of a pregnant woman are of great interest (especially perhaps to those who can never experience them directly), the poem seems to be a valuable psychological and physiological document. But I suggest that it can only be that because it is first a poem, because the writer is able to stand outside her experience and record it in expressive rhythms and images:

> *A creel of eels, all ripples.*

The experience is not uncommon, but the skill in communicating it is.

Knowledge of a poem's origins may add to our appreciation, but we should not use this knowledge as a criterion of the poem's value. Would it alter the poems if we found that Celia once existed outside *Volpone*, or that Jonson really did love a Charis when he was fifty?[2] The mere existence of dramatic poetry is a reminder that 'sincerity' can be no criterion. Even many lyrical pieces, including Jonson's poems to Celia when read in *The Forrest* and not in *Volpone*, are dramatic utterances: the poet speaks with a voice suitable to the role he is adopting.

It is true that poets themselves often talk as though their poetry were the volcanic eruption of forces which, being subterranean, are beyond their control. It is very fashionable now to speak in this way;

---

1. Sylvia Plath, 'You're', *Ariel*, 1965, p. 57.
2. *Let it not your wonder move,*
Lesse your laughter; that I love.
Though I now write fiftie yeares,
I have had, and have my Peeres...
'*His Excuse for loving*', Herford, VIII, 131.

authors often seem to disclaim all knowledge of why they wrote as they did, to imply that – far from intending, with a consciousness of what they were doing and great skill in the doing of it, to make a lucid statement or arouse a particular response in the reader – they were impelled to write, preferably despite themselves, by a strong emotion which they could not, any more than anyone else, possibly understand until it was expressed, if then.[1] It must be remembered too that the idea of a poet as a man who is somehow inspired, and without control over his inspiration, goes back at least to Plato and is found among Jonson's contemporaries. It was in answer to contemporary mockery of Jonson's slow and considered artistry that Carew wrote:

> *Repine not at Thy Tapers thriftie waste,*
> *That sleekes thy tearser Poems; nor is haste*
> *Prayse, but excuse...*[2]

Sometimes a writer may stress his experiences and feelings, and sometimes his skill in ordering them artistically: Jonson's contemporaries did not usually think of poetry as a means of self-expression. To put it very briefly, but not I think misleadingly, Renaissance taste enjoyed poems which were unashamedly didactic, which buttonholed the reader and positively insisted on giving him some sound advice, and also poems which, far from offering advice, said very little about anything but said it with style, poems where the artifice was everything. Neither kind of poem has much to do with the common modern demand for poems which reveal the poet's state of mind.[3] There are many Renaissance poems whose authorship is doubtful, and to a modern reader it can be surprising how little this often matters.

Rosemond Tuve, speaking particularly of Renaissance views on imagery, points out that the effectiveness of the finished product was regarded as more important than any ideas the reader might form of the poet's 'sincerity':

Although it is accepted that a vehement 'inward stir' will character-ize the poet's sensibilities as well, discussions are little preoccupied with his feelings, greatly preoccupied with those he will evoke. The critical question of 'sincerity' is neglected in favor of the poetic

---

1. Lerner, *op. cit.*, p. 38.
2. 'To Ben Johnson vppon occasion of his Ode to Himself', Herford, XI, 336.
3. Douglas Bush, *Classical Influences in Renaissance Literature*, p. 34.

problem of efficacy through credibility. The truth of the affections was a serious matter, but it stood to be answered less in terms of the question 'did the poet feel it?' than 'will the reader feel it and why should he?'[1]

Jonson puts it more tersely:

> *Let me be what I am, as* Virgil *cold ;*
> *As* Horace *fat*; *or as* Anacreon *old ;*
> *No Poets verses yet did ever move,*
> *Whose Readers did not* thinke *he was in love.*[2]

Here we may of course wonder what happens to what Rosemond Tuve calls 'efficacy through credibility'[3] when the poet is so frank about his attempts to be persuasive. The answer is that we believe in the situation of the poet self-consciously moving into action:

> *Who shall forbid me then in Rithme to bee*
> *As light, and active as the youngest hee*
> *That from the Muses fountaines doth indorse*
> *His lynes, and hourely sits the Poets horse?*
> *Put on my Ivy Garland, let me see*
> *Who frownes, who jealous is, who taxeth me.*[4]

One of the greatest dangers in demanding 'sincerity' from a poet is that we are likely to oversimplify the complexity of the feeling in his poem.

This danger is most apparent, I think, when we consider Renaissance commendatory poems, especially funeral elegies. We think of the extravagant praise usual in such pieces, and – ignoring the question of whether the writer himself believed it was true – we ask whether we find it credible, and then often enough decide we do not:

> *'Twere time that I dy'd too, now shee is dead,*
> *Who was my* Muse, *and life of all I sey'd,*

---

1. Tuve, pp. 182–3. A footnote to p. 182 says: 'Sincerity is sometimes commented on, by both theorists and poets, as a prerequisite for writing credibly; Sidney's "look in thy heart and write" is a statement on method and is so presented.'

2. '*An Elegie*', Herford, VIII, 199. I have romanized 'thinke'.

3. Tuve, p. 182.

4. '*An Elegie*', Herford, VIII, 200. See also p. 51 below.

The Spirit that I wrote with, and conceiv'd ;
All that was good, or great in me she weav'd,
And set it forth; the rest were Cobwebs fine,
Spun out in name of some of the old Nine!
To hang a window, or make darke the roome,
Till swept away, th⟨ey⟩ were cancell'd with a broome !
Nothing, that could remaine, or yet can stirre
A sorrow in me, fit to wait to her !
O ! had I seene her laid out a faire Corse,
By Death, *on* Earth, *I should have had remorse*
On Nature, *for her : who did let her lie,*
And saw that portion of her selfe to die.
Sleepie, or stupid Nature, couldst thou part
With such a Raritie, *and not rowse* Art
With all her aydes, to save her from the seize
Of Vulture death, *and those relentlesse cleies ?*
Thou wouldst have lost the Phoenix, *had the kind*
Beene trusted to thee : not to't selfe assign'd.
Looke on thy sloth, and give thy selfe undone,
(For so thou art with me) now shee is gone.
My wounded mind cannot sustaine this stroke,
It rages, runs, flies, stands, and would provoke
The world to ruine with it; in her Fall,
I summe up mine owne breaking, and wish all.
Thou hast no more blowes, Fate, *to drive at one :*
What's left a Poêt, *when his* Muse *is gone ?*[1]

The last line is patently untrue, since the poet is still writing. Jonson told Drummond that he had discussed this kind of writing with Donne, and my impression is that, when he quoted Donne's comment, it was with approval :

> that Dones Anniversarie was profane and full of Blasphemies that he told Mr Donne, if it had been written of ye Virgin Marie it had been something to which he answered that he described the Idea of a Woman and not as she was.[2]

Whether or not Jonson approved of this answer (and his objection had been to profanity rather than exaggeration), it certainly provides

---

1. '*Elegie on my Muse*', Herford, VIII, 282–3.
2. *Conversations,* Herford, I, 133.

a justification for his own extravagant praise of Lady Venetia Digby. It was, in fact, the usual justification offered for poems such as this:

> ... for *Flattery*, no man will take *Poetry literal*; since in *commendations*, it rather shows what men should be, then what they are.[1]

And the poet was not only presenting an ideal; he was also writing for an occasion on which high praise was demanded for politeness' sake: we still take obituaries with a grain of salt. Can we fairly object that such poems are 'insincere', we who say 'Good morning' whatever the weather, and 'How nice to see you' even (or particularly) when it is not nice?

Along with the desire for 'sincerity' goes the desire for 'spontaneity', and both lead to a distrust of the part played by intellect in poetry:

> His throne is not with the Olympians but with the Titans; not with those who share the divine gifts of creative imagination and inevitable instinct, but with those who compel our admiration by their untiring energy and giant strength of intellectual muscle. What we most marvel at in his writings, is the prodigious brain-work of the man, the stuff of constant and inexhaustible cerebration they contain.[2]

The contrast between 'divine gifts' and 'untiring energy' is made here much too glibly, I think.

> It is characteristic of him to believe that the brain first must do all it can and that only when human intellect has reached its height, is it transfigured and carried into the incomprehensible realm of poetry.[3]

This is nearer the mark, but even here it seems to be regarded as strange, if not reprehensible, that Jonson should emphasize the brain-work behind his poetry.

Does this merely exemplify the tendency, natural enough to readers who are not poets, to regard creative power as a blessing, as against the tendency of poets themselves to regard it as something

---

1. Felltham's *Resolves*, 1620, quoted by B.C. Clough, *The Metaphysical Poets*, 1920, p.52.

2. Symonds, p. 198.

3. E.C. Dunn, *Ben Jonson's Art: Elizabethan Life and Literature as Reflected Therein*, 1963 (copyright 1925), p. 91.

more like a curse? It is not surprising that poets should be more conscious of the difficulties and responsibilities of their craft than their readers are, that a poet more modest than Jonson should even blame himself for falling short of his own ideal:

> *... I relapse into my crimes:*
> *Time and again have slubbered through*
> *With slip and slapdash what I do,*
> *Adopted what I would disown,*
> *The preacher's loose immodest tone ;*
> *Though warned by a great sonneteer*
> *Not to sell cheap what is most dear,*
> *Though horrible old* Kipling *cried*
> *'One instant's toil to Thee denied*
> *Stands all eternity's offence,'*
> *I would not give them audience.*
> *Yet still the weak offender must*
> *Beg still for leniency and trust*
> *His power to avoid the sin*
> *Peculiar to his discipline.*[1]

Even in this one short passage we find support for Jonson from a number of poets. The fact remains, however, that Jonson has been criticized more often than most poets for his conscious, meticulous workmanship. Castelain says, rather mysteriously:

Si les mots n'étaient contradictoires en apparence, on pourrait l'appeler le poète du bon sens.[2]
(If the words did not seem to be contradictory, one might call him the poet of good sense.)

One thinks of Dryden, Pope, Samuel Johnson, and Roy Fuller and one wonders why it should be considered strange for a poet to show some commonsense.

There is nothing accidental in the work of Ben Jonson: no casual inspiration, no fortuitous impulse, ever guides or misguides his genius aright or astray.[3]

---

1. W.H. Auden, *New Year Letter*, 1941, lines 218–32, p. 24.
2. Castelain, pp. 849–50.
3. Swinburne, p. 9.

This is more appreciative, certainly, but there is still the implication that something is lacking; what that something is we may guess if we think of Swinburne's own verse. Gregory Smith makes the objection explicit:

> It seems so useless to look for the lyrical note and the abandon of the poet in the analyst and scholar.[1]

Symonds, Castelain, Swinburne, and Smith value what one of them achieved – 'the abandon of the poet'. Here I take a thought from Castelain and suggest that the words 'abandon' and 'poet' are contradictory. Later, Gregory Smith shows more appreciation of Jonson's manner when he says of the best of the *Epigrammes*:

> It is chiselled work, brief in compass, often a restoration rather than an adaptation of old models in motive and phrase, restrained and orderly in its expression, drawn as a cameo or panel is, not wantonly as the graffiti of free passion. In a word, it is classical in origin and nature, and always at its best when frankest in confessing that tradition.[2]

Nevertheless, Smith is suspicious of anything that seems conscious or conscientious in a poem:

> . . . even in his best passages he is interested only in 'literary' values . . . with all his art in transferring or transforming the good things of classical or humanist thought, he seldom gives that spiritual suggestion which in master-verse lies behind the magic of phrase and rhythm. That magic is too often with him merely the legerdemain of style, ingenious, sometimes elegant, but a conjurer's rather than a magician's mystery.[3]

Smith goes on to say that this 'fault', or virtue as I shall try to show it is, is only to be expected when we know something of Jonson's method of composition; he also mentions Jonson's habit of reworking his own phrases.[4] The latter is an economy that many poets have practised (similar to their habit of reworking other people's phrases), and it seems to me evidence only of skill and tenacity – 'Myself must

---

1. Smith, p. 213.
2. *Ibid.*, p. 217.
3. *Ibid.*, p. 243.
4. *Ibid.*, pp. 243–4.

I remake'.[1] Jonson's method of composition, however, suggests what his rejection of 'the graffiti of free passion' means.

Smith is referring, of course, to one of the remarks made to Drummond:

> his opinion of Verses
> that he wrott all his first jn prose, for so his master Cambden had Learned him.[2]

This must be the worst sin of all to anyone who looks for 'abandon' in a poet. It is, of course, the result rather than the method which matters, but – if the objection is made that bad methods lead to bad results – it is worth mentioning as a sufficient reply to Smith that Jonson is here in very good company:

> ... poets as diverse as Virgil, Jonson, Pope, Goldsmith, Coleridge, Tennyson, Browning, Rossetti, and Yeats have all drafted a prose version of what they wanted to say and have later set it out in a metrical pattern.[3]

All the same, this practice of Jonson's does suggest a quality in his work not found in that of all the poets whom Press mentions. Not only the method, but the finished products too, have a deliberation and reasonableness which some will find objectionable. There is no doubt, as the word 'deliberation' suggests, that this is intended. Douglas Bush has noticed in Jonson 'a touch of the Goth',[4] and there is also a comment by Drummond which reminds us that the sobriety of the poems was the result of great effort. He says that Jonson was

> oppressed with fantasie, which hath ever mastered his reason, a generall disease jn many poets.[5]

Much of the attraction of Jonson's poems, especially the lyrics, lies in their shapeliness and finish, in our awareness of the artistic control that has been exercised in making them. The question is how highly we should value these qualities, or rather whether we tend nowadays to undervalue them. R. S. Walker says that the hostility of nineteenth-century critics was the result of

1. W. B. Yeats, 'An Acre of Grass', *Collected Poems*, 1950, p. 346.
2. *Conversations*, Herford, I, 143.
3. John Press, *The Fire and the Fountain*, 1955, p. 164.
4. *Mythology and the Renaissance Tradition in English Poetry*, 1932, p. 215.
5. *Conversations*, Herford, I, 151.

a scale of values based on the apparent spontaneity of the emotion expressed in poetry.[1]

The key-word here is 'apparent', for the essence of Walker's defence of Jonson's lyric poetry is that it does not try even to seem spontaneous:

> . . . his rarest singing lyrics make no attempt to disown their conscious engineering of design.[2]

Some contemporaries could praise Jonson for the very quality which made others so suspicious. Richard West, contrasting Jonson with those who wrote rapidly and easily, says with approval:

> Thine *are the* Works *of* judgement, *theirs of* chance.[3]

There are many pleasures to be gained from reading a good poem, and one of them can be the feeling of admiration for a job well done. This will imply some knowledge of what skill is required, and some sense in the poem of difficulties overcome. The poem will display the mastery of its maker and not try to disguise it.

John Hollander shows himself aware that the demand for 'spontaneity' was not merely a nineteenth-century aberration (though he seems unaware of how old the belief in inspiration is) when he says, after mentioning Jonson's habit of writing prose drafts of his poems:

> It is only the romantic belief that poetry is somehow inspired and mysteriously spontaneous, or the post-symbolist insistence that a poem must *be* its own meaning, scheme and purpose, rather than having separable skeleton, flesh and organs, that can make us blush for Jonson at such a remark.[4]

Far from speaking of poetry as 'mysteriously spontaneous', Jonson suggests a way of working which involves the dissection of a poem into 'separable skeleton, flesh and organs':

> *For* a man to write well, there are required three Necessaries. To read the best Authors, observe the best Speakers: and much exercise of his owne style. In style to consider, what ought to be

---

1. Walker, p. 181.
2. *Ibid.*, p. 187.
3. Richard West, 'On Mr Ben Iohnson', Herford, XI, 469.
4. Hollander, *op. cit.*, p. 10.

written; and after what manner; Hee must first thinke, and excogitate his matter; then choose his words, and examine the weight of either. Then take care in placing, and ranking both matter, and words, that the composition be comely; and to doe this with diligence, and often. No matter how slow the style be at first, so it be labour'd, and accurate: seeke the best, and be not glad of the forward conceipts, or first words, that offer themselves to us, but judge of what wee invent; and order what wee approve.[1]

We see here how 'labour'd' was a word expressing admiration in Jonson's day: the change to the modern meaning marks a change in the attitude towards literature. The aim of the method which Jonson outlines is to produce poems that will compliment the reader by asking to be read with care, studied, and examined for evidence of skill:

A man should so deliver himselfe to the nature of the subject, whereof hee speakes, that his hearer may take knowledge of his discipline with some delight: and so apparell faire, and good matter, that the studious of elegancy be not defrauded ...[2]

To Jonson the poet is not a wild man to wonder at, and to excuse for eccentricity because his very nature implies eccentricity, but one whose inborn gift is so rare and valuable that he has a duty not to abuse it; he is 'y^t kind of artificer, to whose worke is requir'd so much exactnesse, as indifferency is not tolerable'.[3]

Jonson's poems, then, often read as though they were deliberately worked out, and they invite us to do the same. We are invited to pause and deliberate, to judge the worth of what is being said and of how it is being said, to criticize in fact. Jonson does not want a passive reader or one swept off his feet; he wants one competent to judge and discriminate, one who is willing to learn from the poems how to judge and discriminate.

To my meere English Censvrer

To thee, my way in Epigrammes *seemes new,*
When both it is the old way, and the true.
Thou saist, that cannot be: for thou hast seene

---

1. *Discoveries,* Herford, VIII, 615.
2. *Ibid.,* 566–7.
3. *The Masqve of Qveenes,* Herford, VII, 288, note p.

> *Davis, and Weever, and the best haue beene,*
> *And mine come nothing like. I hope so. Yet,*
> *As theirs did with thee, mine might credit get:*
> *If thou'ldst but vse thy faith, as thou didst then,*
> *When thou wert wont t⟨o⟩' admire, not censure men.*
> *Pr'y thee beleeue still, and not iudge so fast,*
> *Thy faith is all the knowledge that thou hast.*[1]

We notice the sudden, unexpected turn on 'I hope so' which makes us compare Jonson's epigrams with Davis's and Weever's and decide between them, and the explanation of why Davis's and Weever's epigrams were popular in the distinction between 'admire' and 'censure' ('wonder at' and 'judge') with its implied general literary value-judgement, and the contrast between 'faith' and 'knowledge' in the last line. The movement of the poem is carefully controlled: a phrase is emphasized by being placed at the end of a line and on a rhyme ('and the true'), the central thought is emphasized by being contained in a very short sentence ('I hope so'), and enjambement (lines 3–5) and the running of a sentence over several lines (lines 5–8) have the effect of slowing down the reading to make it more careful, while the last line is allowed to run out freely as a rapid summary of what has gone before. We are asked to weigh the words in this poem, and to find them worth weighing, to judge the disposition of them and then admire it.

That Jonson in 'To my meere English Censvrer' is using words with exactness can hardly be disputed; but of course a lexicographer may do this. We expect a poet to multiply ambiguities, not remove them:

> . . . while Jonson's use of words is always precise, vigorous and meaningful, he almost always brings into play only their immediate denotatory or 'dictionary' significance, and only rarely calls up their complete range of suggestion, evocation or emotive power. His verse, that is, lacks texture or richness of overtone and verbal harmony, and it is this that distinguishes it so sharply from the work of most of our major poets, and especially from the poetry of Shakespeare.[2]

There is much truth in this, and it can easily be illustrated:

---

1. Herford, VIII, 32.
2. Bamborough, *op. cit.*, p. 33.

On the Vnion
When was there contract better driuen by Fate?
Or celebrated with more truth of state?
The world the temple was, the priest a king,
The spoused paire two realmes, the sea the ring.[1]

This is neat, precise, and adequate to its social purpose of celebrating a public event; but it does not reverberate with suggestiveness. It is not meant to: even the conceit in the last two lines has nothing metaphysical about it; it is there to give a sense of finality, to imply that the last word has been said on the subject. The conceit is, then, suitable to the thoughts and feelings aroused by the event itself, but no more than suitable. This poem, it is true, does not represent Jonson at his best, but it is fairly typical of his style.

It is not that Jonson cannot command sensuous and evocative imagery: he can, but he will do so only when it suits his purpose, for the aptness is all. There are the strange and haunting lines from the poem to Wroth:

Or, if thou list the night in watch to breake,
A-bed canst heare the loud stag speake;[2]

some very sensuous lines from a poem to Charis:

Chin, as woolly as the Peach ...
Skin as smooth as any rush,
And so thin, to see a blush
Rising through it e're it came;[3]

or even something of a metaphysical touch in the description of the progress of a disease:

What could their care doe 'gainst the spight
Of a Disease, that lov'd no light
Of honour, nor no ayre of good?
But crept like darknesse through his blood?[4]

or, on one of his favourite themes, there is 'holiest friend-ship, naked

---

1. Herford, VIII, 28.
2. *Ibid.*, 97.
3. '*Her man described by her owne Dictamen*', *ibid.*, 141.
4. '*An Epitaph, on* Henry L. La-ware', *ibid.*, 234.

to the touch'[1] which illustrates what Eliot admires so much in the Metaphysicals, the 'quality of transmuting ideas into sensations'.[2]

He could be sensuous and evocative when he wished, but usually he did not wish. When Jonson was writing there was not the emphasis there is now on the image as the essence of poetry, something with an almost magical power in itself. I think this emphasis can easily lead us to overestimate the value of sensuousness and evocativeness. Jonson's discussion of the 'three Necessaries'[3] for the writer makes it plain that he saw meaning as coming first, and then the appropriate words with their images:

> Hee must first thinke, and excogitate his matter; then choose his words, and examine the weight of either.[4]

The order of priorities may sound strange to a modern, but it is worth consideration.

There is a strong tendency in modern verse, noticeable at least as early as Hölderlin and very striking in the Symbolists, to deny or ignore the distinction which Jonson takes for granted between matter and words. Decorum, in the sense of choosing the image appropriate to the thought, is seldom mentioned. Frequently, not only logic and consistency of detail, but also all attempt at rational discourse, are abandoned quite deliberately. Again and again we hear that poetry originates in the unconsciousness and irrational, sometimes with the implication that it ought to remain true to its origins and not invade the realm of the conscious and rational. There are no doubt strong reasons for all this: perhaps it is part of a reaction against what are thought to be the more reasonable and intelligible methods of physical science (itself thought to be hostile to poetry), perhaps it is the desire to shock readers thought to be indifferent to poetry, or perhaps merely a feeling that none of this matters much when so few will read the poem. Yet, even if we agree that poetry cannot be explained, or even understood, by the reason alone, we may argue that the reason should not be left out; poetry may appeal to it as well as to other faculties. The characteristic faults of modern poetry are just those faults which Jonson was least ready to tolerate: obscurity, lack

---

1. 'To the same' (Benjamin Rudyerd), *ibid.*, 78.
2. 'The Metaphysical Poets', *Selected Essays*, third edition 1951, p. 290. Essay first published 1921.
3. Quoted above, p. 38.
4. *Discoveries*, Herford, VIII, 615.

of decorum in the imagery, and the tendency for poems to finish up as piles of glittering bric-à-brac rather than clearly-ordered structures with every part contributing to a whole which is intelligible to the reason though not to be exhausted by it.[1] I am reminded of one of Puttenham's definitions:

> . . . figure it selfe is a certaine liuely or good grace set vpon wordes, speaches and sentences to some purpose and not in vaine, giuing them ornament or efficacie by many maner of alterations in shape, in sounde, and also in sence . . .[2]

Puttenham repeats this definition when he says:

> . . . a figure is euer vsed to a purpose, either of beautie or of efficacie . . .[3]

Jonson had read Puttenham, of course,[4] and he used evocative imagery only when his theme required it. His practice is as far as it is possible to be from that of the Symbolists, so neatly defined by Edmund Wilson:

> . . . what the symbols of Symbolism really were, were metaphors detached from their subjects – for one cannot, beyond a certain point, in poetry, merely enjoy color and sound for their own sake: one has to guess what the images are being applied to.[5]

It is worth quoting one well-known Symbolist poem if only to emphasize what Jonson was not trying to do:

> Le vierge, le vivace et le bel aujourd'hui
> Va-t-il nous déchirer avec un coup d'aile ivre
> Ce lac dur oublié que hante sous le givre
> Le transparent glacier des vols qui n'ont pas fui !
>
> Un cygne d'autrefois se souvient que c'est lui
> Magnifique mais qui sans espoir se délivre
> Pour n'avoir pas chanté la région où vivre
> Quand du stérile hiver a resplendi l'ennui.

---

1. C. Day Lewis, *The Poetic Image*, 1947, pp. 114–15.
2. George Puttenham, *The Arte of English Poesie*, ed. Willcock and Walker, 1936, p. 159; first published 1589.
3. *Ibid.*, p. 202.
4. Herford, 1, 264, mentions a copy of Puttenham as one of the books in Jonson's library.
5. *Axel's Castle*, 1931, p. 21.

Tout son col secouera cette blanche agonie
Par l'espace infligée à l'oiseau qui le nie,
Mais non l'horreur du sol où le plumage est pris.

Fantôme qu'à ce lieu son pur éclat assigne,
Il s'immobilise au songe froid de mépris
Que vêt parmi l'exil inutile le Cygne.[1]

(The virginal, lively, and beautiful today, will it rend for us with a blow of its drunken wing this hard, forgotten lake haunted beneath its frost by the transparent glacier of flights that have not flown! A swan of former times remembers that it is he, magnificent but freeing himself without hope for not having sung the region in which to live when the boredom of sterile winter shone. His whole neck will shake off this white agony inflicted by space on the bird which denies it, but not the horror of the earth where his plumage is caught. Phantom whose pure brilliance assigns him to this place, he is motionless in the cold dream of scorn which the Swan wears in his useless exile.)

The immense suggestiveness of this poem comes from the fact that its subject is never overtly stated but has to be inferred from the images; this means that the reader supplies what is to a large extent his own subject for the poem. Mallarmé illustrates here both the triumph and the limitations of the symbolist method. With Jonson we are left in no doubt as to what the subject is:

Goodyere, I' am glad, and gratefull to report,
  My self a witnesse of thy few dayes sport:
Where I both learn'd, why wise-men hawking follow,
And why that bird was sacred to Apollo,
Shee doth instruct men by her gallant flight,
  That they to knowledge so should toure vpright,
And neuer stoupe, but to strike ignorance:
  Which if they misse, they yet should re-aduance
To former height, and there in circle tarrie,
  Till they be sure to make the foole their quarrie.
Now, in whose pleasures I haue this discerned,
  What would his serious actions me haue learned?[2]

---

1. *Poésies de Stéphane Mallarmé*, Librairie Gallimard, 1945, pp. 123–4.
2. 'To Sir Henry Goodyere', Herford, VIII, 55.

As Trimpi says:

> The bird's movements reflect perfectly the classical ideal of exploration and the subsequent recovery of a flexible position from which new exploration can be made.[1]

Mallarmé intrigues by his obscurity, and Jonson amazes by his clarity.

The difference, however, is not merely one between an emphasis on 'style' and an emphasis on 'meaning' such as Edward B. Partridge mentions:

> Some rhetoricians in the eighteenth century thought that the vehicle could be detached and that the tenor – 'the plain meaning' – – was all that finally mattered. Such ignoring of the vehicles obviously results in an impoverishment of the poetic experience. But in some modern studies of imagery there is the reverse practice of thinking that the only thing that really matters is the vehicle and that the tenor can be detached.[2]

As Partridge says:

> The trouble is that this concern with either tenor or vehicle alone is artistically irrelevant. A statistical listing of either metaphor or vehicle which neglects the use of a metaphor in a certain situation by a certain person ignores the only relationships which matter: that is, the interaction between tenor and vehicle, and the relation between the metaphor and its context.[3]

Rosemond Tuve makes the same point:

> I have encountered no early discussion of metaphor which falls into the modern habit of emphasizing the nature of *that to which* the comparison is made; the emphasis even in the most pedestrian of handbook writers is upon pleasure in the nature of the 'affinity' seen.[4]

I suggest that our pleasure in Jonson's image of the hawk comes precisely from our recognition of this 'affinity' between the theme

---

1. Trimpi, p. 174.
2. Partridge, *op. cit.*, p. 30.
3. *Ibid.*, p. 31.
4. Tuve, p. 121.

and the movements of the bird. I shall even go further and suggest that, although it is common nowadays to admire images when they become identified with what they express, we can only take pleasure in the 'affinity' between two things as long as we are still aware that they are different. The detachability of the images from the theme may then become one criterion of a poem's merit.

At least I think it leads to a better appreciation of Jonson's poetry if we regard his images, even when they are evocative ones, as chiefly remarkable for their precise definition of moral qualities:

> *And hath the noblest marke of a good Booke,*
> *That an ill man dares not securely looke*
> *Vpon it, but will loath, or let it passe,*
> *As a deformed face doth a true glasse;*[1]

or of moral and emotional states:

> *'Twill see it's sister naked, ere a sword.*[2]

Even when, as in his comparison between 'A *Bed-rid* Wit' and 'a *besieged* Towne',[3] Jonson uses the highly technical language appropriate to the vehicle, he does not let it obscure the tenor. The sardonic humour of this comparison depends on our being kept aware that it is a comparison:

> Disease, *the Enemie, and his Ingineeres,*
> Want, *with the rest of his conceal'd compeeres,*
> *Have cast a trench about mee, now, five yeares*;
>
> *And made those strong approaches, by* False braies,
> Reduicts, Halfe-moones, Horne-workes, *and such close wayes,*
> *The* Muse *not peepes out, one of hundred dayes . . .*[4]

By the way in which he uses his imagery Jonson reminds us of the English Augustan poets, and he has often been compared to them in other respects also. I suppose no one would deny that Jonson played a major part in the development of the heroic couplet.[5] The

1. '*On the Author, Worke, and Translator*', Herford, VIII, 389.

2. 'On the Townes Honest Man', Herford, VIII, 74.

3. '*To the Right Honourable, the Lord high Treasurer of* England. *An Epistle Mendicant*', *ibid.*, 248.

4. *Ibid.*

5. Douglas Bush, *English Literature in the Earlier Seventeenth Century 1600–1660*, p. 104.

terms in which he expressed his preference for this verse-form
foreshadow its later development and dominance. His proposed epic
was

> all jn Couplets, for he detesteth all other Rimes, said he had written
> a discourse of Poesie both against Campion & Daniel especially
> this Last, wher he proves couplets to be the bravest sort of Verses,
> especially when they are broken, like Hexameters and that crosse
> Rimes and Stanzaes (becaus the pūrpose would lead him beyond
> 8 lines to conclude) were all forced.[1]

In more subtle ways too his verse looks forward to that of the
Augustans. F. R. Leavis, discussing 'the line of wit',[2] says:

> The line, then, runs from Ben Jonson (and Donne) through Carew
> and Marvell to Pope.[3]

The danger in emphasizing Jonson's influence is that he may be
regarded merely as a precursor of the Augustans, someone who
inaugurated a manner without perfecting it. His poetry is of value in
itself; it is not merely a half-way house between the Romans (especially Horace and Martial) and the climax of English verse satire in
Pope. T. K. Whipple distinguishes neatly between Jonson and
Martial, but fails to distinguish adequately between Jonson and
Pope:

> In style, Jonson approaches Martial, but does not give an exact
> English equivalent of the Latin. For Jonson's divergences, two
> reasons may be offered. In the first place, he was among the first in
> England to practise that balanced and antithetic style, imitated
> from the Latin poets, which found its greatest master in Pope; we
> could not expect a beginner to exhibit complete mastery. In the
> second place, the temper of Jonson's mind did not permit him to
> achieve the lightness of Martial. His expression is heavier,
> weightier, graver, than Martial's.[4]

I do not think that Jonson was aiming at 'the lightness of Martial'
or, although he is in the same tradition as Pope, at the sort of lightness

---

1. *Conversations*, Herford, I, 132.
2. Leavis, *op. cit.*, pp. 17–41.
3. *Ibid.*, p. 29.
4. *Martial and the English Epigram from Sir Thomas Wyatt to Ben Jonson*, 1925, p. 403.

and delicacy which Pope achieved. This tendency to denigrate Jonson in contrast with Pope is seen again in Ronald Duncan's introduction to his selection. After quoting in full the poem 'To Fine Lady Wovld-bee'[1] (a poem which he obviously admires very much, since he gives it again in full in the body of the selection), he writes:

> In such polished verses, which Jonson considered mere tavern trifles one can, I think, see the beginnings of Augustan wit and urbanity crystallizing. The very run of Pope's couplet is anticipated here.[2]

That Jonson regarded such poems as 'mere tavern trifles' is, of course, untrue; but to offer such an excuse is hardly less depreciatory than to praise for 'the beginnings of Augustan wit and urbanity'.

Jonson's poetry does indeed lack those qualities for which we most value the Augustans. A passage from Jonson's 'To the World' at first pleases by its simple and adequate statement of a noble sentiment:

> *But, what we' are borne for, we must beare:*
> *Our fraile condition it is such,*
> *That, what to all may happen here,*
> *If't chance to me, I must not grutch.*
> *Else, I my state should much mistake,*
> *To harbour a diuided thought*
> *From all my kinde: that, for my sake,*
> *There should a miracle be wrought.*[3]

But if we go to Samuel Johnson, we cannot fail to see what has been gained in conciseness and wit:

> *Yet hope not life from grief or danger free,*
> *Nor think the doom of man revers'd for thee.*[4]

A comparison between Jonson and Pope, when they are both re-working a familiar passage from Horace,[5] is not so damaging to Jonson. His version has considerable force:

---

1. Herford, VIII, 46.
2. *Selected Poems of Ben Jonson*, 1949, p. 16.
3. Herford, VIII, 101.
4. '*The Vanity of Human Wishes*', lines 155–6, *The Poems of Samuel Johnson*, ed. Smith and McAdam, 1941, pp. 37–8.
5. *Ep.* II. i. 114–7, *Horace. Satires, Epistles and Ars Poetica*, with English translation by H. Rushton Fairclough, 1926, p. 406.

> *You learn'd it well; and for it, seru'd your time*
> *A Prentise-ship: which few doe now a dayes.*
> *Now each Court-Hobby-horse will wince in rime;*
> *Both learned, and vnlearned, all write* Playes.
> *It was not so of old: Men tooke vp trades*
> *That knew the Crafts they had bin bred in, right:*
> *An honest* Bilbo-*Smith would make good blades,*
> *And the* Physician *teach men spue, or shite;*
> *The* Cobler *kept him to his nall*; *but, now*
> *Hee'll be a* Pilot, *scarce can guide a Plough.*[1]

But even this, fine as it is with its 'surly virtue'[2] relieved by a touch
of humour, is bare-fist fighting in comparison with Pope. Pope's
version is lighter in tone and its wit, especially in the second line, is
deadly:

> *He serv'd a 'Prenticeship, who sets up shop;*
> *Ward try'd on Puppies, and the Poor, his Drop;*
> *Ev'n Radcliff's Doctors travel first to France,*
> *Nor dare to practise till they've learn'd to dance.*
> *Who builds a Bridge that never drove a pyle?*
> *(Should Ripley venture, all the World would smile)*
> *But those who cannot write, and those who can,*
> *All ryme, and scrawl, and scribble, to a man.*[3]

We cannot help noticing, too, that Pope's lines are more complex
than Jonson's; Pope is not making, as Jonson is, a simple contrast
between high standards of craftsmanship in the past and low standards
in the present: he is satirizing everyone he mentions.

Pope's superiority over Jonson in this kind of satire, where the
victim becomes 'the sad Burthen of some merry Song',[4] is obvious.
What I suggest is that Jonson was not usually trying for the same
effects as Pope. What he was trying to do is mentioned by Kathryn
McEuen when she says of '*An Epistle to a Friend, to perswade him
to the Warres*'[5] that 'it contains exhortation; and the tone is that of

---

1. 'To my old Faithfull Seruant: and (by his continu'd Vertue) my louing Friend: the Author of this Work, M. Rich. Brome', Herford, VIII, 410.

2. Samuel Johnson, 'LONDON', line 45, *op. cit.*, p. 16.

3. '*The First Epistle of the Second Book of Horace Imitated*', lines 181–8, *The Poems of Alexander Pope*, 1963, ed. Butt, p. 642.

4. '*The First Satire of the Second Book of Horace Imitated*', *ibid.*, p. 616.

5. Herford, VIII, 162.

invective',[1] or when she says, comparing Jonson with Juvenal:

> Jonson seldom laughs, unless it be in savage glee as he drives home a thrust. But this is not Horace's way of laughing.[2]

It is not Pope's or Dryden's way of laughing either. Again, Kathryn McEuen says that, unlike Martial who was able to laugh at vice, Jonson 'censured bitterly'.[3]

The difficulty, when we try to distinguish Jonson from Pope, lies I think in the word 'satire' which almost inevitably makes us think of what satire means with Pope. I think it is usually better to use the words 'invective' and 'denunciation' when speaking of Jonson. He seldom preserves the poker-face of Dryden or Pope; often he frowns in anger and threatens:

> *What is't, fine Grand, makes thee my friendship flye,*
> *Or take an* Epigramme *so fearefully:*
> *As't were a challenge, or a borrowers letter?*
> *The world must know your greatnesse is my debter.*
> In-primis, *Grand, you owe me for a iest,*
> *I lent you, on meere acquaintance, at a feast . . .*
> *Fortie things more, deare Grand, which you know true,*
> *For which, or pay me quickly', or Ile pay you.*[4]

Sometimes Jonson laughs, but it is usually a belly-laugh of sheer delight at his victim's discomfiture:

> *Shift, here, in towne, not meanest among squires,*
> *That haunt* Pickt-hatch, Mersh-Lambeth, *and* White-fryers,
> *Keepes himselfe, with halfe a man, and defrayes*
> *The charge of that state, with this charme, god payes.*
> *By that one spell he liues, eates, drinkes, arrayes*
> *Himselfe: his whole reuennue is, god payes . . .*
> *But see! th'old baud hath seru'd him in his trim,*
> *Lent him a pockie whore. Shee hath paid him.*[5]

A similar joke provokes a similar laugh in 'On English Movnsievr':

---

1. *Classical Influence upon the Tribe of Ben*, 1939, p. 46.
2. *Ibid.*, p. 49.
3. *Ibid.*, p. 16.
4. 'To Fine Grand', Herford, VIII, 51.
5. 'On Lievtenant Shift', *ibid.*, 30–1.

Would you beleeue, when you this Movnsievr see,
  That his whole body should speake french, *not he?*
That so much skarfe of France, *and hat, and fether,*
  And shooe, and tye, and garter should come hether,
And land on one, whose face durst neuer bee
  Towards the sea, farther then halfe-way tree? ...
Or had his father, when he did him get,
  The french *disease, with which he labours yet?*[1]

None of this is subtle: it appeals by its directness and force. Whereas Pope and Dryden usually inflict their wounds without warning, Jonson (as I have said) frequently threatens, and the appeal of some of his poems lies in the threat rather than its carrying out:

Sʳ Inigo doth feare it as I heare
(And labours to seem worthy of yᵗ feare)
That I should wryte vpon him some sharp verse,
Able to eat into his bones & pierce
The Marrow![2]

Of course, the satiric point of that poem lies in its contemptuous refusal to satirize; but Jonson obviously enjoys displaying himself as a dangerous man to cross:

Put on my Ivy Garland, let me see
Who frownes, who jealous is, who taxeth me.[3]

This attitude is a favourite one with Catullus too, and it is worth quoting him here to show the sort of comparison which I think helps us to appreciate Jonson's manner:

quare aut hendecasyllabos trecentos
expecta aut mihi linteum remitte ...[4]

(Therefore, either send me back my napkin, or look out for three hundred hendecasyllabics ...)

and

---

1. *Ibid.*, 56.
2. 'To affreind an Epigram of him', *ibid.*, 407–8.
3. '*An Elegie*', *ibid.*, 200. See also p. 32 above.
4. Catullus, No. XII, pp. 16–18.

> *Qvaenam te mala mens, miselle Ravide,*
> *agit praecipitem in meos iambos?*[1]

(What wrongheadedness, wretched Ravidus, makes you rush to get in the way of my iambics?)

and

> *Adeste, hendecasyllabi, quot estis*
> *omnes undique, quotquot estis omnes.*[2]

(Come here, hendecasyllabics, from everywhere, all that there are of you, all of you as many as there are.)

So Jonson falls short *'if to laugh and rally is to be preferr'd to railing and declaiming'*[3] for he can seldom hold himself back from trying 'to lash the Ideots into Sence'.[4] Nevertheless, *'railing and declaiming'* has its own appeal; appreciation is largely a matter of enjoying what is there, without repining for what is not there and is not meant to be there. If we look for some tradition of poetry in English in which to place Jonson's invective, we can find respectable company for him. A poem like Ralegh's 'The Lie' has the same directness and plain, unsubtle force:

> *Say to the Court it glowes,*
> *and shines like rotten wood,*
> *Say to the Church it showes*
> *whats good, and doth no good.*
> *If Church and Court reply,*
> *then giue them both the lie.*[5]

In Milton also there is sometimes the same fierce denunciation, made more fierce occasionally by sardonic humour:

> *But we do hope to find out all your tricks,*
> *Your plots and packings wors then those of Trent,*
> *That so the Parlament*
> *May with their wholsom and preventive Shears*
> *Clip your Phylacteries, though bauk your Ears,*

---

1. Catullus, No. XL, p. 46.

2. Catullus, No. XLII, p. 48.

3. Preface to *Sylvae, The Poems of John Dryden*, ed. J. Kinsley, I, 1958, p. 399. Dryden is comparing Horace to Juvenal.

4. Anon, *'The Tory-Poets: a Satyr'* (1682), Herford, XI, 546. The writer is suggesting how Jonson would have treated contemporary poetasters.

5. *The Poems of Sir Walter Ralegh*, ed. Agnes Latham, 1951, p. 45.

And succour our just Fears
When they shall read this clearly in your charge,
New Presbyter *is but* Old Priest *writ Large*.[1]

The Bible, of course, contains much invective, in prose, as in Ezekiel's attack on 'the shepherds of Israel':

Ho, shepherds of Israel who have been feeding yourselves! Should not shepherds feed the sheep? You eat the fat, you clothe yourselves with the wool, you slaughter the fatlings; but you do not feed the sheep...[2]

and in verse, as in Isaiah's denunciation of 'the daughters of Zion':

The Lord said:
Because the daughters of Zion are haughty
and walk with outstretched necks,
glancing wantonly with their eyes,
mincing along as they go,
tinkling with their feet ;
the Lord will smite with a scab
the heads of the daughters of Zion,
and the Lord will lay bare their secret parts.[3]

It will be noticed that Isaiah's notion of poetic justice is similar to Jonson's.[4] To mention only one more example out of many, the attack on idolatry in Psalm CXXXV shows a scorn reminiscent of Jonson:

The idols of the nations are silver and gold,
the work of men's hands.
They have mouths, but they speak not,
they have eyes, but they see not,
they have ears, but they hear not,
nor is there any breath in their mouths.
Like them be those who make them ! –
yea, every one who trusts in them ![5]

---

1. '*On the new forcers of Conscience under the Long* PARLAMENT', *Milton's Poetical Works*, ed. H. Darbishire, II, 1955, p. 157.
2. *Ezekiel*, xxxiv. 2–3, Revised Standard Version.
3. *Isaiah*, iii. 16–17, *ibid*.
4. As in 'On Lievtenant Shift', lines 23–4, quoted above, p. 50.
5. 15–18, Revised Standard Version.

I hope that, in my disagreement with what seem to me unprofitable ways of approaching Jonson's poetry, I have not given the impression that I regard him as a faultless writer. Douglas Bush, suggesting some of the virtues we can find in Jonson, does not make any allowance for Jonson's failures:

> Reacting against the Elizabethan vagaries of matter, form, and style, Jonson demanded, and unceasingly strove for, the ageless classical virtues of clarity, unity, symmetry, and proportion; in short, the control of the rational intelligence. His poems are wholes, not erratic displays of verbal fireworks, and false taste always pronounces such writing 'barren, dull, leane'.[1]

This is a fine description of Jonson's qualities when he is at his best, but, as Bradbrook points out:

> When Jonson is not at his best, his poems are too elaborate, lacking in spontaneity and flexibility, clumsy and harsh.[2]

I am dubious what 'lacking in spontaneity' means, but the rest of it is a fair comment on Jonson's failures. Wesley Trimpi gives a set of faults to which a writer like Jonson is most liable:

> Barrenness, dullness, and leanness are the faults that the plain style is most likely to fall into, according to every rhetorical treatise.[3]

Jonson did not always manage

> to avoid the sin
> Peculiar to his discipline.[4]

An instance of 'barrenness, dullness, and leanness' is the poem 'On Mill my Ladies Woman'[5] which seems to have no point at all. For Jonson when he is being 'clumsy and harsh' there is the awkward rhythm of the first line of one of his most admired poems:

> See the Chariot at hand here of Love.[6]

---

1. *English Literature in the Earlier Seventeenth Century 1600–1660*, p. 108.
2. Bradbrook, *op. cit.*, p. 136.
3. Trimpi, p. 56. These are the faults Bush mentions above; both writers are remembering *Discoveries*, Herford, VIII, 587.
4. Quoted above, p. 35.
5. Herford, VIII, 57.
6. '*Her Triumph*', *ibid.*, 134.

It is even possible, though this is much more difficult, to find bathos in Jonson, in a couplet surprisingly reminiscent of McGonagall:

> *Witnesse his Action done at* Scandero⟨o⟩ne;
> *Upon my Birth-day the eleventh of* June.[1]

If I prefer to concentrate on Jonson's successes, which incidentally I believe to be far more numerous than his failures, it is because I consider this the best approach for any poet who is worth studying at all. Once a poet's virtues are recognized, his shortcomings become more apparent by contrast.

> The character of the man is clearly reflected in Jonson's writings, and forms by no means their least interesting feature. They . . . are truculent, saturnine, direct, full of arrogance and sincerity, permeated with a love of literature, but without human passion or tenderness . . . He repels his admirers, he holds his readers at arm's length. He is the least sympathetic of all the great English poets, and to appreciate him the rarest of literary tastes is required, – an appetite for dry intellectual beauty, for austerity of thought, for poetry that is logical, and hard, and lusty . . . he made a deep mark on our literature for several generations subsequent to his own, and he enjoys the perennial respect of all close students of poetry.[2]

It seems fitting to quote Edmund Gosse here, particularly since he is not entirely sympathetic to Jonson. His comment summarizes much of the ground covered in this chapter and also points to some that must be covered in the next.

---

1. '*An Epigram To my* MVSE, *the Lady* Digby, *on her Husband, Sir* Kenelme Digby', *ibid.*, 262.
2. Edmund Gosse, *The Jacobean Poets*, 1899, pp. 38–9.

2

'The World's Pure Gold'[1]

In all the variety of Jonson's work, on many subjects and in many manners, there are some themes which he treats again and again, themes with which he was obviously preoccupied and which stirred his imagination more than most. Although Gregory Smith is, I think, unfair to describe Jonson's manner as 'lumbering' in the poems he mentions, he does show that he has reacted to some of the highlights in Jonson's poetry:

> In the epistles of the more ceremonious kind, like those to the Countess of Rutland (*For.* XII.) or to Lady Aubigny (*ib.* XIII.), Jonson writes in a lumbering manner, with now and then a rhetorical ecstasy.[2]

At least two critics find Jonson at his best when he writes of vice and stupidity, and they also use the poem to Lady Aubigny to illustrate their point. Herford and Simpson notice that

> the pace quickens, and a more individual colour comes into the diction, when he turns from direct eulogy to chastise those who praise her for the wrong things, – for the fortune which is irrelevant, or the beauty which any fool can see; and the 'other great wiues' whom her purity and fidelity put to the blush.[3]

Laurence Lerner agrees:

> Jonson's imagination was always caught by ingenious wickedness, and the accents of denunciation move him more than others. So in the middle of this flat epistle an experience stirs – a brief moment of eager castigating of vice, catching some of the colourfulness of what it denounces – rises to intensity, and then gradually subsides back into the poem.[4]

---

1. 'To the same', Herford, VIII, 78.
2. Smith, p. 236.
3. Herford, II, 370.
4. Lerner, *op. cit.*, p. 100.

The passage Lerner quotes is this:

> *Let who will follow fashions, and attyres,*
>   *Maintayne their liedgers forth, for forraine wyres,*
> *Melt downe their husbands land, to poure away*
>   *On the close groome, and page, on new-yeeres day,*
> *And almost, all dayes after, while they liue;*
>   *(They finde it both so wittie, and safe to giue.)*
> *Let 'hem on poulders, oyles, and paintings, spend,*
>   *Till that no vsurer, nor his bawds dare lend*
> *Them, or their officers: and no man know,*
>   *Whether it be a face they weare, or no.*[1]

There is no doubt that this passage is more forceful than the rest of the poem; but it does not break the unity of the poem for, although Jonson here 'turns from direct eulogy', it is so that he may continue the eulogy indirectly. The point is important, I think, because it is not only the spectacle of vice and stupidity which brings out the best in Jonson as a poet. Vice and stupidity interest him, at the same time as they anger him, because they offend against his ideals. Even at his most vituperative it is usually clear that he is writing in defence of his ideals (which are quite definite ones) and of

> *vertue most,*
> *Without which, all the rest were sounds, or lost.*[2]

Of course, as Gilbert Highet remarks, 'all satirists are at heart idealists';[3] but it is particularly important to stress Jonson's idealism, since his satire and denunciation are so often merely incidental to his vigorous and explicit statement of his ideals. Moreover, Jonson is remarkably consistent in what he likes and dislikes, so that a clear recognition of his ideals is a great help to the appreciation of his poetry. He put the mark of his personality and beliefs on almost everything he wrote, with the result that his poems often underline each other – an individual poem tends to gain when read in the context of his whole work. I do not think that detailed discussion of any poet's 'thought', considered apart from all the other elements which go to

---

1. Herford, VIII, 118.
2. *Ibid.*
3. *The Anatomy of Satire*, 1962, p. 243: 'Although some are too embittered, others too convulsed with laughter, to give voice to their positive beliefs, all satirists are at heart idealists.'

make up his poetry, can have much value: poets should not be read as though they were philosophers. All that I shall attempt in this chapter is to indicate Jonson's salient attitudes and those features of his style which seem to me to be conditioned partly by these attitudes. This is as a preliminary to discussing some of the poems in more detail separately, and I think it is a necessary preliminary. If I am right in believing that Jonson's poetry must be seen as a whole, that as a whole it adds up to more than the sum of its parts,[1] and that it is futile to talk of his style apart from his subject matter – then we have good reason to regard him as not merely a good, but a great, poet.

Poets naturally value poetry, but it is doubtful if any ever valued it more highly than Jonson:

> Poets are esteem'd above Princes; I have a reverend Author for it called *Taylor the Water-Poet*;
>
> > When Nature did intend some wond'rous thing,
> > She made a Poet, or at least a King.
>
> *Ben. Johnson* wou'd a given a hundred pounds (if he had had it, that is) to have been Author of those two lines.[2]

Jonson made up for not writing those two lines by writing many others very like them. One reason he valued poetic ability so highly was that he was convinced

> *That* Poets *are far rarer births then kings.*[3]

He told Prince Henry:

> *Poetry*, my Lord, is not borne wth euery man; Nor euery day . . .[4]

Frequently this idea is expressed with the incidental satire so typical of his work:

> They [poets] are not borne euerie yeere, as an Alderman.[5]

We find the same sort of thing in *Discoveries* when Jonson is speaking

---

1. T. S. Eliot tentatively suggests this as a test of major poetry in his essay 'What is Minor Poetry?', *On Poetry and Poets*, 1957, p. 47. This essay was first published in 1944.

2. John Lacy, *Sir Hercules Buffoon* (1684), Herford, XI, 546.

3. 'To Elizabeth Covntesse of Rvtland', Herford, VIII, 53.

4. Dedication, '*The Masqve of Qveenes*', Herford, VII, 281.

5. *Every Man in his Humour*, V. v. 38–9, Herford, III, 400; I quote the revised version from the Folio of 1616.

of the great natural abilities and conscientious dedication required of a poet:

> Every beggerly Corporation affoords the State a *Major*, or two *Bailiffs*, yearly: but, *solus Rex, aut Poeta, non quotannis nascitur.*[1]

Again and again, as in the two odes to himself[2] or the poem to the Countess of Rutland,[3] Jonson rises to the heights when he expresses his sense of the nobility of the poet's vocation. Some of his most fervent lines are those which show what pleasure it gave him to be equal to the severe demands of his craft:

> *Looser-like, now, all my wreake*
> *Is, that I have leave to speake,*
> *And in either Prose, or Song,*
> *To revenge me with my Tongue,*
> *Which how Dexterously I doe,*
> *Heare and make Example too.*[4]

In such passages the poet seems to be amazed at his own skill, and the result is an exhilarating sense of sheer delight in creative ability, a delight far removed from mere arrogance or conceit. It is in this way that I interpret Fabian's remark in the middle of one of the most skilfully funny scenes in *Twelfth Night*:

> If this were played upon a stage now, I could condemn it as an improbable fiction.[5]

Jonson valued poetry not only because it was rare (so was the gold he so much despised), but also because he believed that only poetry could celebrate goodness and greatness as they should be celebrated and preserve for posterity the fame of those who deserved fame. In a poem attacking the King's household for not giving him his yearly allowance of sack, he warns:

> *... in the Genius of a Poets Verse,*
> *The Kings fame lives. Go now, denie his Teirce.*[6]

---

1. Herford, VIII, 637.
2. Herford, VIII, 174; Herford, VI, 492.
3. Especially lines 41–63, Herford, VIII, 114–15.
4. '*What hee suffered*', *ibid.*, 133.
5. III. iv. 133–4, ed. Morton Luce, 1906, p. 120.
6. Herford, VIII, 241.

Poetry is valued partly because of the value of what it can celebrate:

> *It is not growing like a tree*
> *In bulke, doth make man better bee ;*
> *Or standing long an Oake, three hundred yeare,*
> *To fall a logge at last, dry, bald, and seare:*
> *A Lillie of a Day,*
> *Is fairer farre, in May,*
> *Although it fall, and die that night;*
> *It was the Plant, and flowre of light.*
> *In small proportions, we just beautie see:*
> *And in short measures, life may perfect bee.*[1]

Poems, too, like lives, may be perfect 'In small proportions' and 'in short measures'; in this passage Jonson's two great ideals – of the perfect life and the perfect work – come together. The poem to Sir Henry Savile illustrates well how Jonson particularly admired 'literary skill joined to integrity of character'.[2] Indeed the poem makes it plain that these qualities can hardly be considered separately, since 'integrity of character' is essential for 'literary skill', in this case the skill of the historian:

> *Although to write be lesser then to doo,*
> *It is the next deed, and a great one too.*
> *We need a man that knowes the seuerall graces*
> *Of historie, and how to apt their places ;*
> *Where breuitie, where splendor, and where height,*
> *Where sweetnesse is requir'd, and where weight ;*
> *We need a man, can speake of the intents,*
> *The councells, actions, orders, and euents*
> *Of state, and censure them: we need his pen*
> *Can write the things, the causes, and the men.*
> *But most we need his faith (and all haue you)*
> *That dares not write things false, nor hide things true.*[3]

Jonson does not admire and praise isolated, spectacular successes in a man's life or work so readily as wholeness and completion, an ideal for which the circle is an appropriate image:

---

1. '*To the immortall memorie, and friendship of that noble paire, Sir Lvcivs Cary, and Sir H. Morison*', *ibid.*, 245.
2. Walton, p. 30.
3. Herford, VIII, 61–2.

> *...may all thy ends,*
> *As the beginnings here, proue purely sweet,*
> *And perfect in a circle always meet.*[1]

The image of a pair of compasses is sometimes used to express the physical and mental processes necessary to achieve this ideal:

> *Stand forth my Object, then, you that have beene*
> *Ever at home: yet, have all Countries seene:*
> *And like a Compasse keeping one foot still*
> *Upon your Center, doe your Circle fill*
> *Of generall knowledge...*[2]

A pair of compasses was also Jonson's impress, and Partridge has an interesting comment to make on this:

One symbol of Jonson's sense of perverted values in an age that was a lamentable falling off from the Golden Age was his own imprese. It represented a compass, which Jonson in *The Masque of Beautie* called one of the 'known ensignes of *perfection*'. In this masque the allegorical figure of 'Perfectio' is described as having 'In her hand a *Compasse* of golde, drawing a *circle*'. But in the imprese – and this is the revealing part – the compass is broken, so that the circle is incapable of completion. The motto '*Deest quod duceret orbem*' was adapted from a passage in Ovid's *Metamorphoses* which goes '*altera pars staret, pars altera duceret orbem*'. For Jonson ... one part might stand fixed, but the other part could not describe a circle, for the compass was broken, the circle could never be complete, and perfection was eternally marred here below the moon.[3]

The desire for perfection, whether of a life or of a work, leads so often to disappointment that it is not surprising that many of Jonson's most powerful passages are denunciation of a falling away from this perfection. Indeed, although I do think that in the passage from the poem to Lady Aubigny quoted above[4] Jonson is using denunciation as a means of indirect eulogy, elsewhere it is often difficult to decide

---

1. 'To William Roe', *ibid.*, 81.
2. '*An Epistle to Master* Iohn Selden', *ibid.*, 159.
3. Partridge, *op. cit.*, p. 239. Partridge's footnotes are omitted.
4. P. 57.

whether he is not using eulogy as a means of denunciation. Castelain says of the poem to Rutter:

> Beau morceau si l'on veut, mais moins fait pour être agréable à Rutter que pour dire son fait au public imbécile – ou à quelque rival inconnu.[1]
>
> (A fine piece certainly, but written less to give pleasure to Rutter than to tell the stupid public – or some unknown rival – what he thinks of them.)

Castelain's interpretation is supported by the end of the poem, with its forceful attack on inadequate critics:

> *...Now there is a new*
> *Office of Wit, a Mint, and (this is true)*
> *Cry'd up of late: Whereto there must be first*
> *A* Master-worker *call'd, th'old standerd burst*
> *Of wit, and a new made: a* Warden *then,*
> *And a* Comptroller, *two most rigid men*
> *For order, and for governing the pixe,*
> *A* Say-master, *hath studied all the tricks*
> *Of* Finenesse, *and* alloy *: follow his hint,*
> *Yo'have all the* Mysteries *of* Wits new Mint,
>   *The valuations, mixtures, and the same*
>   *Concluded from a* Carract *to a* dramme.

On the other hand, the direct praise of Rutter's achievement is even more striking, and here again what Jonson praises is the perfection that he finds in wholeness and completion:

> *...I have read,*
> *And weigh'd your* Play *: untwisted evr'y thread,*
> *And know the woofe, and warpe thereof; can tell*
> *Where it runs round, and even: where so well,*
> *So soft, and smooth it handles, the whole piece,*
> *As it were spun by nature, off the fleece:*
> *This is my censure.*[2]

So Jonson tends to be at his best when a consideration of a perfect life or work (especially a literary work, and more especially poetry)

---

1. Castelain, p. 776.
2. Herford, VIII, 415.

is involved, or when he is angered by a falling off from this perfection.

It is a natural result of Jonson's persistent idealism in an imperfect world that one of his commonest ways of praising one person is by dispraising another. Sometimes this dispraise takes up nearly the whole of a complimentary poem, and the compliment has mainly to be understood by contrast:

> *Not he that flies the court for want of clothes,*
> *At hunting railes, hauing no guift in othes,*
> *Cryes out 'gainst cocking, since he cannot bet,*
> *Shuns prease, for two main causes, poxe, and debt,*
> *With me can merit more, then that good man,*
> *Whose dice not doing well, to'a pulpit ran.*
> *No, Shelton, giue me thee, canst want all these,*
> *But dost it out of iudgement, not disease;*
> *Dar'st breath in any ayre; and with safe skill,*
> *Till thou canst finde the best, choose the least ill.*
> *That to the vulgar canst thy selfe apply,*
> *Treading a better path, not contrary;*
> *And, in their errors maze, thine owne way know:*
> *Which is to liue to conscience, not to show.*
> *He, that, but liuing halfe his age, dyes such;*
> *Makes, the whole longer, then 'twas giuen him, much.*[1]

Sometimes the dispraise comes as a mere incidental snarl:

> *This booke! it is a* Catechisme *to fight,*
> *And will be bought of euery Lord, and Knight,*
> *That can but reade...*[2]

Sometimes it comes as a witty interjection intensifying an already complimentary comparison:

> *I confesse all, I replide,*
> *And the Glasse hangs by her side,*
> *And the Girdle 'bout her waste,*
> *All is* Venus: *save unchaste.*[3]

Sometimes praise and dispraise are given equal weight:

---

1. 'To Sir Raph Shelton', *ibid.*, 76.
2. 'THE VISION OF Ben Ionson, ON THE MUSES OF HIS FRIEND M. Drayton', *ibid.*, 398.
3. '*His discourse with* Cupid', *ibid.*, 137.

Stay, view this stone: And, if thou beest not such,
Read here a little, that thou mayst know much.
It couers, first, a Virgin; and then, one
That durst be that in Court: a vertu' alone
To fill an Epitaph.[1]

True to his concern with morals, Jonson is aware of the poet's responsibility to give good measure in his poems by cramming them with meaning. John Beaumont, in his elegy on Jonson, praises Jonson's language in significant terms:

... perhaps some Pedant begs
He may not use it, for he heares 'tis such,
As in few words, a man may utter much.[2]

In his *Discoveries*, after attacking those who write deliberately roughly, Jonson attacks those whose lines are smooth enough yet lack deep meaning:

Others there are, that have no composition at all; but a kind of tuneing, and riming fall, in what they write. It runs and slides, and onely makes a sound. Womens-*Poets* they are call'd: as you have womens-*Taylors*.

They write a verse, as smooth, as soft, as creame;
In which there is no torrent, nor scarce streame.

You may sound these wits, and find the depth of them, with your middle finger. They are *Creame-bowle*, or but puddle deep.[3]

That Jonson uses this image of the cream-bowl in one of his poems also, this time to refer not to a poem but to a lover, shows how he applies similar standards to both art and life:

No, Mistris, no, the open merrie Man
Moves like a sprightly River, and yet can

---

1. 'Epitaph', *ibid.*, 371. This epitaph is on Cecilia Bulstrode who was the victim of '*An Epigram on The Court Pucell*' (*ibid.*, 222) discussed above, pp. 13–15. The contrast between the poems in their attitude to Cecilia Bulstrode is hard to explain (see Herford, XI, 130–1), but it is of interest because it illustrates in an extreme form 'the variety of attitude' to be found in Jonson which is mentioned above, p. 13.

2. Herford, XI, 439.
3. Herford, VIII, 585.

> *Keepe secret in his Channels what he breedes,*
> *'Bove all your standing waters, choak'd with weedes.*
> *They looke at best like Cream-bowles, and you soone*
> *Shall find their depth: they're sounded with a spoone.*[1]

As one example of the terseness Jonson always aimed for and so often achieved, here is one of his poems to Sir Henry Goodyere.[2] In it life and learning are judged by the same standards:

> *When I would know thee Goodyere, my thought lookes*
> *Vpon thy wel-made choise of friends, and bookes;*
> *Then doe I loue thee, and behold thy ends*
> *In making thy friends bookes, and thy bookes friends ...*

The full force of 'know' and 'loue' is only felt when we read the rest of the poem, and particularly the last two lines:

> *Now, I must giue thy life, and deed, the voice*
> *Attending such a studie, such a choice.*
> *Where, though 't be loue, that to thy praise doth moue,*
> *It was a knowledge, that begat that loue.*

The poem is typical of Jonson in that it must be read and appreciated as a whole: he is not a writer who shows at his best, or who even intended to show at his best, in isolated lines and phrases.

The poem to Sir Henry Goodyere is typical too in Jonson's insistence that he knows what he is doing when he gives praise; it is as though he assumes that Goodyere, or anyone else reading the poem, will not allow himself to be carried away by fulsome flattery but will weigh and judge the words used and their appropriateness. It is to emphasize this care and discrimination in his praise that Jonson so often uses comparatives when others might have used superlatives. There is another reason for this habit, of course; Jonson can seldom forbear comparing what he admires with what he considers less admirable. There is, for instance, his address to his book of *Epigrammes:*

> *... by thy wiser temper, let men know*
> *Thou art not couetous of least selfe-fame,*
> *Made from the hazard of anothers shame ...*[3]

---

1. '*An Elegie*', *ibid.*, 198.
2. *Ibid.*, 55.
3. *Ibid.*, 27.

his praise of the Countess of Bedford:

> *I meant each softest vertue, there should meet,*
> *Fit in that softer bosome to reside ...*[1]

and, in the poem 'To Penshvrst':

> *Some bring a capon, some a rurall cake,*
> *Some nuts, some apples; some that thinke they make*
> *The better cheeses, bring'hem ...*[2]

If, as I suggest, much of the power of Jonson's poetry comes from its communication of an interesting and forceful personality, it should be worth while to examine in more detail some of the preoccupations of that personality as they are revealed in the poetry. Robert Bell praises Jonson in terms that are not fashionable nowadays, but he has grasped one of Jonson's chief attractions as a poet:

> The predominant merit of his poems lies in their practical wisdom ... His lines are pregnant with thought applicable to the conduct of life; and without any of the affectation of aphorisms, multitudes of his couplets might be separated from the text, and preserved apart for their axiomatic completeness.[3]

Herford and Simpson express similar views, but emphasize the personal qualities of the writer as they are revealed in his poems. They say that we should not expect even from Jonson's poems in heroic couplets anything like the elegance, the 'smoothness', of Waller. We should not expect these qualities simply because the poems reveal, as they are meant to, Jonson's own temperament which was so very far from being 'smooth'. The poems display Jonson's intellectual grandeur, his noble ideal of manliness, and of course his personal charm.[4] When Jonson praised other poets, it was often in moral terms:

> ... our ablest Judge & Professor of *Poesie*, said with some passion, *My Son* CARTWRIGHT *writes all like a Man:* You'll soon guess 'twas *Ben Iohnson* spake it ...[5]

---

1. *Ibid.*, 52.
2. *Ibid.*, 95.
3. Memoir included in *Poetical Works of Ben Jonson*, 1856, p. 24.
4. Herford, II, 413.
5. Preface to the Reader from William Cartwright's *Comedies, Tragi-Comedies, With other Poems*, 1651, Herford, XI, 504.

For Jonson, literature is less concerned with giving sensuous pleasure than with revealing mental and moral states:

> *My mirror is more subtile, cleere, refin'd,*
> *And takes, and giues the beauties of the mind.*[1]

It is for this reason he values poetry above graphic art:

> ... the Pen is more noble, then the Pencill. For that can speake to the Understanding; the other, but to the Sense. They both behold pleasure, and profit, as their common Object...[2]

Jonson described his *Epigrammes* as '*my* Theater, *where* Cato, *if he liu'd, might enter without scandall*',[3] not merely stressing that his poems were moral, but also suggesting the sort of morality to be found in them. With the mention of Cato we expect an emphasis on Roman virtues, and this expectation is fulfilled when we come to the poems. There is plenty of evidence in them for the assertion that 'the note of a Stoic' is 'the deepest strain of his nature',[4] and not only in the *Epigrammes* but throughout his poetry. Time and again he advises his friends to rely upon themselves and not on the approbation of others:

> *Then stand vnto thy selfe, not seeke without*
> *For fame, with breath soone kindled, soone blowne out.*[5]

He frequently represents himself as one who does not seek applause; his book, he tells his bookseller, must

> *lye vpon thy stall, till it be sought;*
> *Not offer'd, as it made sute to be bought...*[6]

A man must live up to the ideal he sets himself and

> *He that departs with his owne honesty*
> *For vulgar praise, doth it too dearely buy.*[7]

Perhaps the noblest expression of this ideal of self-sufficiency, which

---

1. '*Epistle*. To Katherine, Lady Avbigny', Herford, VIII, 117.
2. *Discoveries, ibid.*, 610.
3. Dedication to *Epigrammes, ibid.*, 26.
4. Herford, II, 375.
5. 'To the same' (Alphonso Ferrabosco), Herford, VIII, 83.
6. *Ibid.*, 28.
7. 'To my Booke', *ibid.*, 27.

of course involves resignation to the suffering of life, comes at the end of 'To the World':

> *Nor for my peace will I go farre,*
> *As wandrers doe, that still doe rome,*
> *But make my strengths, such as they are,*
> *Here in my bosome, and at home.*[1]

These 'strengths' must include a calm acceptance of the transience of life. Many times, and often in almost the same words, Jonson says that life is a debt we must be ready to repay at any time. To his dead son he says:

> *Seuen yeeres tho' wert lent to me, and I thee pay,*
> *Exacted by thy fate, on the iust day.*[2]

To the bereaved parents of the Lady Jane Pawlet he says:

> *Goe now, her happy Parents, and be sad,*
> *If you not understand, what Child you had.*
> *If you dare grudge at Heaven, and repent*
> *T' have paid againe a blessing was but lent,*
> *And trusted so, as it deposited lay*
> *At pleasure, to be call'd for, every day!*[3]

The final blessing he wishes to Sir Robert Wroth is:

> *... when thy latest sand is spent,*
> *Thou maist thinke life, a thing but lent.*[4]

Another striking feature of Jonson's personality, or of his moral values, is his uncompromising, sometimes ruthless, honesty. However much the origins of this quality may have lain in his temperament, it was a quality he admired so much that he fostered it as carefully as he did his stoicism. He told Drummond:

of all stiles he loved most to be named honest, and hath of that ane hundreth letters so naming him.[5]

---

1. *Ibid.*, 102. R. G. Cox ('A Survey of Literature from Donne to Marvell', *A Guide to English Literature*, III, ed. Boris Ford, 1956, p. 53) quotes this passage as an example of 'the Horatian tone of balanced moderation, the quiet acceptance of the human lot'.
2. Herford, VIII, 41.
3. *Ibid.*, 271.
4. *Ibid.*, 100.
5. *Conversations*, Herford, I, 150.

This shows, of course, that he was not so indifferent to outside approval as he would have liked to be, and it reminds us that it is ideals we are concerned with. However, it would be hard to find any poet who was less of a sycophant. It was not an idle boast that

he would not flatter though he saw Death.[1]

This ideal,

Which is to liue to conscience, not to show,[2]

makes Jonson particularly annoyed by all forms of deception, hypocrisy, or pretension. This explains much of his bitterness towards Inigo Jones; Jones designed the settings, the outward show, for their masques, and apparently felt that these were more important than the poetry:

> *Content thee to be Pancridge Earle ye whyle;*
> *An Earle of show: for all thy worke is showe:*
> *But when thou turnst a Reall Inigo;*
> *Or canst of truth ye least intrenchm^t pitch,*
> *Wee'll haue thee styld ye Marquess of New-Ditch.*[3]

Clothing often becomes for Jonson a symbol of deception, a sign of the efforts men and women make to seem better than they really are. For a poet to praise

The Stuffes, the Velvets, Plushes, Fringes, Lace,[4]

and ignore the reality they conceal, is unforgivable:

> *Such Songsters there are store of; witnesse he*
> *That chanc'd the lace, laid on a Smock, to see,*
> *And straight-way spent a Sonnet; with that other*
> *That (in pure Madrigall) unto his Mother*
> *Commended the French-hood, and Scarlet gowne*
> *The Lady Mayresse pass'd in through the Towne,*
> *Unto the Spittle Sermon. O, what strange*
> *Varietie of Silkes were on th'Exchange!*
> *Or in Moore-fields, this other night! sings one,*

1. *Ibid.*, 141.
2. 'To Sir Raph Shelton', Herford, VIII, 76.
3. 'To Inigo Marquess Would be', *ibid.*, 407.
4. '*An Elegie*', *ibid.*, 202.

> *Another answers, 'Lasse, those Silkes are none,*
> *In smiling* L'envoye, *as he would deride*
> *Any Comparison had with his Cheap-side.*[1]

Moral responsibilities remain the same, however much fine clothes and fine words are used to disguise them:

> *She must lie downe: Nay more,*
> *'Tis there civilitie to be a whore;*
> *Hee's one of blood, and fashion! and with these*
> *The bravery makes, she can no honour leese:*
> *To do't with Cloth, or Stuffes, lusts name might merit;*
> *With Velvet, Plush, and Tissues, it is spirit.*[2]

Although G. B. Johnston mentions Camden's essay on clothing and his 'evident disapproval of extravagant and outlandish costume'[3] the idea is of course a common one, and is even, as Puttenham says,

spoken in common Prouerbe.

> *An ape vvilbe an ape, by kinde as they say,*
> *Though that ye clad him all in purple array.*[4]

In Jonson the notion is so common as to be an obsession. When Charis is made to describe her ideal man, she says:

> *Well he should his clothes to⟨o⟩ weare;*
> *Yet no Taylor help to make him;*
> *Drest, you still for man should take him;*[5]

and, amongst many other examples, there is the attack 'On English Movnsievr':

> *. . . is it some* french *statue? No: 'T doth moue,*
> *And stoupe, and cringe. O then, it needs must proue*
> *The new* french-*taylors motion, monthly made,*
> *Daily to turne in Pavls, and helpe the trade.*[6]

---

1. *Ibid.*, 201–2.
2. '*An Epistle to a Friend, to perswade him to the Warres*', ibid., 163–4.
3. *Ben Jonson: Poet*, 1945, p. 74.
4. Puttenham, *op. cit.*, p. 201.
5. '*Her man described by her owne Dictamen*', Herford, VIII, 141.
6. *Ibid.*, 56.

The fop described in 'On the new Motion' seems to have no reason for his pride:

> *What then so swells each lim?*
> *Onely his clothes haue ouer-leauen'd him.*[1]

Cosmetics come under attack for the same reason. Particularly when he was with courtiers, Jonson was interested

> *to know*
> *Whether their faces were their owne, or no.*[2]

As with everything he disliked, Jonson shows considerable technical knowledge:

> *She never sought*
> *Quarrell with Nature, or in ballance brought*
> *Art, her false servant; Nor, for Sir Hugh Plat,*
> *Was drawne to practise other hue, then that*
> *Her owne bloud gave her: Shee ne're had, nor hath*
> *Any beliefe, in Madam Baud-bees bath,*
> *Or Turners oyle of Talck. Nor ever got*
> *Spanish receipt, to make her teeth to rot.*[3]

Social rank too, like clothes and cosmetics, might be a disguise for a man's lack of true worth, and Jonson, who 'never esteemed of a man for the name of a Lord',[4] was just as severe to this form of deception as to any other. A poet's function is not the same as a herald's:

> *May none, whose scatter'd names honor my booke,*
> *For strict degrees of ranke, or title looke:*
> *'Tis 'gainst the manners of an* Epigram:
> *And, I a* Poet *here, no* Herald *am.*[5]

Even when virtue and blood come together in the same person – and

---

1. *Ibid.*, 63.
2. '*An Elegie*', *ibid.*, 200.
3. '*An Epigram. To the small Poxe*', *ibid.*, 188. The references to 'Madam Baud-bees bath' and the 'Spanish receipt' have not been identified. I think the latter is probably an allusion to poems xxxix and xxxvii of Catullus (Catullus, p. 46 and p. 44) which contain attacks on the Spaniard Egnatius 'opaca quem bonum facit barba/et dens Hibera defricatus urina' (made fine by a dark beard and by teeth rubbed with Spanish urine), No. xxxvii. 19–20.
4. *Conversations*, Herford, I, 141.
5. 'To all, to whom I write', Herford, VIII, 29.

Jonson complimented very many titled people in his poems – it is the virtue that is admired:

> *Hang all your roomes, with one large Pedigree:*
> *'Tis Vertue alone, is true Nobilitie.*[1]

Again, when he is describing the kind of person he would like to 'honor, serue, and loue', he says:

> *I meant to make her faire, and free, and wise,*
> *Of greatest bloud, and yet more good then great . . .*[2]

The poem 'To Sir Henry Nevil' is worth quoting in full since it combines many features typical of Jonson's poetry – his evaluation of virtue above rank, his love of honesty and dislike of ostentation (particularly in dress), his insistence that life is only lent to us, his tendency to praise one person by disparaging another, and his conviction that it was an important function of poetry to preserve the fame of virtue for posterity:

> *Who now calls on thee, Nevil, is a* Muse,
> *That serues nor fame, nor titles; but doth chuse*
> *Where vertue makes them both, and that's in thee:*
> *Where all is faire, beside thy pedigree.*
> *Thou art not one, seek'st miseries with hope,*
> *Wrestlest with dignities, or fain'st a scope*
> *Of seruice to the publique, when the end*
> *Is priuate gaine, which hath long guilt to friend.*
> *Thou rather striu'st the matter to possesse,*
> *And elements of honor, then the dresse;*
> *To make thy lent life, good against the* Fates:
> *And first to know thine owne state, then the States.*
> *To be the same in roote, thou art in height;*
> *And that thy soule should giue thy flesh her weight.*
> *Goe on, and doubt not, what posteritie,*
> *Now I haue sung thee thus, shall iudge of thee.*
> *Thy deeds, vnto thy name, will proue new wombes,*
> *Whil'st others toyle for titles to their tombes.*[3]

---

1. '*To* Kenelme, Iohn, George', *ibid.*, 282.
2. 'On Lvcy Covntesse of Bedford', *ibid.*, 52.
3. *Ibid.*, 70.

Jonson never tries to disguise the didactic intention of most of his poetry; indeed he emphasizes it. Sometimes he even uses descriptive names for those whom he denounces. Perhaps the most striking of these names is 'Sir Volvptvovs Beast'[1] which suggests in the surname the sordid reality of the sin whose attractiveness has already been suggested in the Christian (or perhaps it would be more accurate to say fore-) name. The most terse of these names is the simple 'Gvt';[2] but the best are those which, while still descriptive of moral qualities, might plausibly be the victims' real names – 'Chev'rill the Lawyer',[3] 'Lievtenant Shift',[4] or 'Captaine Hazard'.[5] The chief purpose of all the names is to ensure that, whatever the initial impetus to make the poem may have been, the attack in it is on a type rather than an individual.

Although Jonson's victims are usually presented as types, and seldom given their real names (even Inigo Jones is sometimes given the doubtful benefit of a descriptive phrase[6]), his heroes and heroines are real people and their praise is particularized and personal:

> *He that should search all Glories of the Gowne,*
> *And steps of all rais'd servants of the Crowne,*
> *He could not find, then thee, of all that store*
> *Whom Fortune aided lesse, or Vertue more.*
> *Such,* Coke, *were thy beginnings, when thy good*
> *In others evill best was understood:*
> *When, being the Strangers helpe, the poore mans aide,*
> *Thy just defences made th'oppressor afraid.*
> *Such was thy Processe, when Integritie,*
> *And skill in thee, now, grew Authoritie;*
> *That Clients strove, in Question of the Lawes,*
> *More for thy Patronage, then for their Cause,*
> *And that thy strong and manly Eloquence*
> *Stood up thy Nations fame, her Crownes defence.*[7]

---

1. *Ibid.*, 34.
2. *Ibid.*, 76.
3. *Ibid.*, 38 and 44.
4. *Ibid.*, 30.
5. *Ibid.*, 56. There is some evidence that names tended to be more obviously descriptive and colourful in Jonson's day than they do in ours. See Marchette Chute, *Ben Jonson of Westminster*, 1954, p. 215.
6. As in 'On the Townes honest Man', Herford, VIII, 74, which is clearly an attack on Inigo Jones. See Herford, XI, 26.
7. '*An Epigram on Sir* Edward Coke, *when he was Lord chiefe Iustice of* England', Herford, VIII, 217.

Similarly the types Jonson attacks are carefully placed in the England, and usually in the London, of their day. Even here, then, the general statements in the poems are particularized by frequent references, often detailed ones, to the life of the time. Jonson's idealism was not starry-eyed: he found it justified by the lives of some of his acquaintances, and it even survived his detailed observation of people like 'Lievtenant Shift'[1] in his natural surroundings of '*Pickt-hatch, Mersh-Lambeth*, and *White-fryers*' where he eats at 'ordinaries', dices, and 'takes up fresh commoditie', and whence he crosses the Thames to the theatres outside the city-limits where, although he is one of the audience, he 'adornes the stage'. The main criticism of Shift, as of so many people in Jonson's poems, is that he is a hypocrite. This criticism is particularized by the reiteration of a phrase in common use at the time, a phrase which lent itself easily to hypocrisy – 'god payes'.

With the frequent local and contemporary references goes a colloquial, idiomatic way of writing. Jonson agreed with Puttenham that a poet's language should 'be naturall, pure, and the most vsuall of all his countrey';[2] he said in *Discoveries:*

> Pure and neat Language I love, yet plaine and customary. A barbarous Phrase hath often made mee out of love with a good sense; and doubtfull writing hath wrackt me beyond my patience.[3]

Another passage in *Discoveries* shows that Jonson's dislike of what was unusual in diction and idiom was part of his dislike of all pretentiousness:

> But now nothing is good that is naturall: Right and naturall language seem⟨s⟩to have least of the wit in it; that which is writh'd and tortur'd, is counted the more exquisite. Cloath of Bodkin, or Tissue, must be imbrodered; as if no face were faire, that were not pouldred, or painted? No beauty to be had, but in wresting, and writhing our owne tongue? Nothing is fashionable, till it bee deform'd; and this is to write like a *Gentleman*. All must bee as affected, and preposterous as our Gallants cloathes, sweet bags,

---

1. *Ibid.*, 30.
2. Puttenham, *op. cit.*, p. 144.
3. Herford, VIII, 620.

and night-dressings: in which you would thinke our men lay in, like *Ladies:* it is so curious.[1]

The avoidance of affectation was a moral responsibility for the poet, and so was the avoidance of obscurity, to which affectation and pretentiousness could so easily lead:

Metaphors farfet hinder to be understood, and affected, lose their grace.[2]

As Jonson puts it in verse:

Lesse shall I for the Art or dressing care,
Truth, and the Graces best, when naked are.[3]

We shall not be disappointed if we look in Jonson for what Donald Davie has called a

strength of statement [which] is found most often in a chaste or pure diction, because it goes together with economy in metaphor; and such economy is a feature of such a diction. It is achieved by judgement and taste, and it preserves the tone of the centre, a sort of urbanity. It purifies the spoken tongue, for it makes the reader alive to nice meanings.[4]

It is understandable that a contemporary like John Beaumont should say that Jonson

made our Language pure and good,
To teach us speake, but what we understood,[5]

or that another contemporary, Henry King, should speak of

that Spring,
To whose most rich and fruitfull head we owe
The purest streams of language which can flow.[6]

---

1. *Ibid.*, 581.
2. *Ibid.*, 621.
3. '*An Epistle to Master* Iohn Selden', *ibid.*, 158.
4. *Purity of Diction in English Verse*, 1952, p. 68. On the previous page Davie credits Jonson with 'this nicety of statement'.
5. In his elegy on Jonson, Herford, XI, 438.
6. In his elegy on Jonson, *ibid.*, 440.

What is more difficult to account for is the attractiveness of such a bare, unadorned way of writing. Wesley Trimpi says:

> The unspecialized, styleless style, whose models are the familiar letter and urbane conversation, is by definition incapable of predication. It is characterized mainly by what it should avoid.[1]

There is much truth in this; nevertheless, poetry is not made simply by avoiding faults. Although Jonson despised 'dressing' he was really far from despising 'Art', and his art must be discussed. Barish suggests an approach which reminds us again of the importance of the subject matter in Jonson:

> Jonson's poems have been misunderstood and underrated. In their avoidance of the expected splendors and excitement of language, their refusal to enchant or ravish, their stubborn, scrupulous effort to render certain kinds of moral experience, his poems remain unread . . .[2]

The essence of Jonson's style is that it is meant to suit its subject matter; like the historian, the poet must know

> *Where breuitie, where splendor, and where height,*
> *Where sweetnesse is requir'd, and where weight.*[3]

To illustrate what I think Barish means by Jonson's 'scrupulous effort to render certain kinds of moral experience', I shall take first a few lines from a love poem:

> *I will not stand to justifie my fault,*
> *Or lay the excuse upon the Vintners vault;*
> *Or in confessing of the Crime be nice,*
> *Or goe about to countenance the vice,*
> *By naming in what companie' twas in,*
> *As I would urge Authoritie for sinne.*[4]

---

1. Trimpi, p. 58. See Yvor Winters, 'The Sixteenth Century Lyric in England', an essay in three parts, *P.C.* (February, March, April 1939), for an attempt to place Jonson in an English tradition of plain writing: 'His style is on the whole plain and direct, but it is likewise polished and urbane. It shows the solid substructure of Gascoigne and Raleigh, with at least evidence of a knowledge of the flexibility of Sidney' (Part III, p. 41).
2. Review of Trimpi, *M.P.*, LXI No. 3 (February 1962), 240.
3. 'To Sir Henrie Savile', Herford, VIII, 62.
4. '*An Elegie*', *ibid.*, 191.

The language here is 'plaine and customary', but lifted above the usual by its precision in revealing the psychology of a guilty person; in the last line the thought reaches a climax by stressing the absurdity of any attempt to excuse himself. There is wit here, but it is not ostentatious.

One of Jonson's best poems, a poem apparently so simple in expression that it is very difficult to analyse,[1] illustrates very well what effect can be gained by a careful defining and qualifying in the poem of the words used in it. The result is a precise estimation of moral qualities. I quote the poem in full, romanizing the parts which particularly show this defining and qualifying process at work:

Epitaph on Elizabeth, L. H.

Would'st thou heare, what man can say
      In a little ? *Reader, stay.*
Vnder-neath this stone doth lye
      As much beautie, as could dye:
Which in life did harbour giue
      To more vertue, then doth liue.
If, at all, *shee had a fault,*
      Leaue it buryed in this vault.
One name was Elizabeth,
      Th'other let it sleepe with death:
Fitter, *where it dyed, to tell,*
      Then that it liu'd at all. *Farewell.*[2]

It is in this sense of careful discrimination, particularly in moral matters, that I interpret Peter Heylyn's description of Jonson as 'equall to any of the antients for the exactness of his Pen'.[3] That this sort of discrimination was a habit with Jonson, even in his conversation, is clear from many of his remarks to Drummond, especially his evaluations of his wife as 'a shrew yet honest'[4] and of Samuel

---

1. George Williamson praises this poem particularly for its reticence. After mentioning Cleveland's epitaph on Strafford, he says: 'Another example of riddling elegiac epigram is Jonson's "Epitaph on Elizabeth, L. H.".... In neither case is it easy to "let it sleep with death".' (*The Proper Wit of Poetry*, 1961, pp. 77–8.) There is an interesting analysis by Howard S. Babb, 'The "Epitaph on Elizabeth, L. H." and Ben Jonson's Style', *J.E.G.P.*, LXII (1963), 738–44.

2. Herford, VIII, 79.

3. *Cosmographie*, 1652, Herford, XI, 504.

4. *Conversations*, Herford, I, 139.

Daniel as 'a good honest Man . . . bot no poet'.[1] Again and again we find Jonson balancing one word against another and consequently one set of values against another, as in the second line of 'To Fine Lady Wovld-bee' where 'make' is contrasted with 'beare':

> *Fine Madame Wovld-bee, wherefore should you feare,*
> *That loue to make so well, a child to beare?*[2]

or in the last two lines of 'To the learned Critick' where 'giuen' is contrasted with 'stolne' and 'sprigge' with 'gyrlands':

> *And, but a sprigge of bayes, giuen by thee,*
> *Shall out-liue gyrlands, stolne from the chast tree.*[3]

Sometimes alliteration is used to connect two words so that the development of meaning in the second one is stressed, as with 'doe' and 'dare' here:

> *A lord, it cryed, buried in flesh, and blood,*
> *And such from whom let no man hope least good,*
> *For I will doe none: and as little ill,*
> *For I will dare none. Good Lord, walke dead still.*[4]

Sometimes words even more closely connected in sound are used, so that the similarity in sound highlights the difference in sense:

To Foole, or Knave

> *Thy praise, or dispraise is to me alike,*
> *One doth not stroke me, nor the other strike.*[5]

Sometimes Jonson exploits an ambiguity to reveal how different our attitudes can be to the same thing, and to point the difference between the appearance and the inner reality of a person. He asks 'Madame Wovld-bee' why she prefers to use an abortifacient rather than bear a child:

> *Will it hurt your feature?*
> *To make amends, yo' are thought a wholesome creature.*[6]

---

1. *Ibid.*, 132.
2. Herford, VIII, 46.
3. *Ibid.*, 32.
4. 'On some-thing, that walkes some-where', *ibid.*, 30.
5. *Ibid.*, 46.
6. *Ibid.*

The ambiguity lies, of course, in 'wholesome' which can mean both physical attractiveness and moral goodness. Sometimes a Latinate pun, as here with a play on the two senses of '*securely*' (carelessly and safely), after a play on the similarity of sound between 'sense' and 'sentence', contrasts appearance with reality:

> *And to his sense obiect this sentence euer,*
> Man may securely sinne, but safely neuer.[1]

A similarity between phrases may be used to emphasize a difference in moral connotations:

> *...what the golden age did hold*
> *A treasure, art: contemn'd in th' age of gold.*[2]

Often Jonson uses a straightforward pun (if a pun is ever straightforward):

> *Groyne, come of age, his state sold out of hand*
> *For' his whore: Groyne doth still occupy his land.*[3]

Even in this poem, which is far from subtle, the pun on 'occupy' is not simply a cheap joke. If we read it in the context of some of Jonson's other poems, particularly 'To Penshvrst'[4] and 'To Sir Robert Wroth',[5] with their praise of the right use of land, the way in which it can be fruitfully occupied, we are more aware of Groyne's perverted sense of values in selling his land to buy a whore.

To some there may seem a lack of naturalness in Jonson's punning, for there are those who object to puns on principle. Among them is Dryden, who objects particularly to Jonson's using puns when speaking in his own person and not through a dramatic character. Dryden says that Jonson

> was not free from the lowest and most groveling kind of wit, which we call clenches . . . This was then the mode of wit, the vice of the Age, and not *Ben. Johnson's*, for you see, a little before him, that admirable wit, Sir *Philip Sidney*, perpetually playing with his words . . .[6]

---

1. 'Epode', *ibid.*, 113.
2. 'To the same. *Vpon the accession of the Treasurer-ship to him*', *ibid.*, 47.
3. 'On Groyne', *ibid.*, 75.
4. *Ibid.*, 93.
5. *Ibid.*, 96.
6. *Defence of the Epilogue to The Conquest of Granada*, 1672, Herford, XI, 526.

I have always found Dryden's consistent dislike of puns surprising. I should have thought that puns, when they are unforced (as Jonson's always are except when he wants a comic effect), would have appealed to Dryden as a means of bringing together in one word two different areas of thought and contrasting them:

> *Play-wright me reades, and still my verses damnes,*
> *He sayes, I want the tongue of* Epigrammes;
> *I haue no salt: no bawdrie he doth meane.*
> *For wittie, in his language, is obscene.*[1]

The use of puns seems to me a natural consequence of an interest in words and meanings and a desire for exactness in their use. Hugh Kenner makes an interesting comment on Donne's use of puns which could be applied just as well to Jonson's:

Donne's readers . . . did not feel as we do that a word's identity is inextricable from its spelling; hence the naturalness, in their utterances, of what we uncomfortably feel to be 'puns'. 'Sun' and 'son' are for us two different words which sound alike; so are 'Donne' and 'done'; and we think a writer who exploits the similarity of sound does something brash and a little disreputable. For the seventeenth century Dean of St Paul's, however, 'sunne' was imprimis an *utterance*, vocalic not typographic, which in denoting both the Second Person of God and the fire of heaven touched on a mystery distinctions of spelling might analyse but not resolve; his great 'Hymne to God the Father' does not so much play upon words as meditate on such mysteries.[2]

Suitable to a colloquial diction is a rhythm which matches that of speech, and this Jonson normally uses. This does not mean that he breaks up the metre, as Donne sometimes does for dramatic effect: it means that, while maintaining the metre, he still manages to give his lines the feel of speech, and of forceful and energetic speech.[3] Jonson's dislike of 'what is rough, and broken' must not be taken, therefore, as a recommendation of mere smoothness for its own sake; the objection, as so often, is to ostentation and eccentricity:

---

1. 'To Play-wright', Herford, VIII, 42.
2. Editor's Note to *Seventeenth Century Poetry, The Schools of Donne and Jonson*, 1964, p. x.
3. Cox, *op. cit.*, p. 53.

Others, that in composition are nothing, but what is rough, and broken . . . And if it would come gently, they trouble it of purpose. They would not have it run without rubs, as if that stile were more strong and manly, that stroke the eare with a kind of uneven⟨n⟩esse. These men erre not by chance, but knowingly, and wittingly; they are like men that affect a fashion by themselves, have some singularity in a Ruffe, Cloake, or Hat-band . . .[1]

Jonson's verse is not rough, but Swinburne accuses it of a worse defect:

Donne is rugged: Jonson is stiff. And if ruggedness of verse is a damaging blemish, stiffness of verse is a destructive infirmity. Ruggedness is curable; witness Donne's *Anniversaries*: stiffness is incurable; witness Jonson's *Underwoods*.[2]

There may be stiffness to be found in Jonson's verse, but it is not usual. What I think Swinburne is really objecting to is that Jonson did not write like Swinburne: Jonson adjusts his rhythm to mark the progress of his thought. Wesley Trimpi illustrates this by Jonson's 'To Heaven'[3] which must, of course, be read as a whole to see the force of what Trimpi says:

Despite the extreme use of *commata*, the rhythm of the verse does not become violent, because there is a cautiously observed gradation in the weight and duration of the pauses and because the majority of the caesuras are extremely light. They slow the line down but do not stop it abruptly. This constant restraint suggests the existence of a continual, underlying movement, which requires control; it takes great skill to achieve the quietness of tone without losing the rhythmical life of the line.[4]

In short, the rhythm follows the movement of the poet's thought:

If a poet's chief concern is with content, he will choose the form that is most flexible and most adaptable to his subject matter. This is the most important single reason why Jonson adopted the couplet and rejected the sonnet.[5]

---

1. *Discoveries*, Hertford, VIII, 585.
2. Swinburne, p. 99.
3. Herford, VIII, 122.
4. Trimpi, pp. 130–1.
5. *Ibid.*, p. 105.

The same principles are observed when Jonson is not writing in couplets, as Trimpi shows by his comment on the poem 'High-spirited friend...':[1]

> However elegant in diction, it is the constantly changing relation between the syntactical units and the length of the lines which gives to the poem an informal flexibility consistent with its purpose of friendly admonishment.[2]

The violence of the enjambement in the poem to Sir Lucius Cary and Sir Henry Morison is unusual in Jonson:

> ... there he lives with memorie; and *Ben*

The Stand

> Jonson, *who sung this of him, e're he went*
> *Himselfe to rest,*
> *Or taste a part of that full joy he meant*
> *To have exprest,*
> *In this bright* Asterisme:
> *Where it were friendships schisme,*
> (*Were not his* Lucius *long with us to tarry*)
> *To separate these twi-*
> Lights, the Dioscuri;
> *And keepe the one halfe from his* Harry.[3]

John Hollander shows that even this violence has a purpose, although I do not think the result is so successful as he does:

> ... the 'twin lights' are separated, by the enjambement of the line, from the unified word 'twilights' in which they were joined. Here the meter imitates the action of death by cutting the word apart even as death divided the two men. In the previous stanza, Jonson has also employed a striking enjambement ... The strophe ends: 'And there he lives with memorie: and *Ben*', and there one tends to come to a full stop. But the next strophe begins '*Jonson*, who sung this of him, e're he went/Himselfe to rest'. This is no arbitrary shock, but is again a kind of pun-by-discovery. Just '*Ben*' may

---

1. Herford, VIII, 180.
2. Trimpi, p. 198.
3. Herford, VIII, 246.

appear over-familiar; but with the addition of the enjambed line, the poet, as he would have been known by the living Cary, the late Morison, and the whole 'Tribe of Ben' becomes the public figure, the author of the *Works*. Thus is the poem labeled with the poet's dual name, expressing his private and public roles and duties.[1]

We can, I think, see Jonson's command of expressive rhythm and his use of the verse-form to emphasize his meaning most easily in a poem which has few other attractions, where the rhythm is almost all that makes the poem attractive. Such a poem is the one Jonson wrote for the portrait of Shakespeare included in the First Folio:

To the Reader

> *This Figure, that thou here seest put,*
> *It was for gentle Shakespeare cut;*
> *Wherein the Grauer had a strife*
> *With Nature, to out-doo the life:*
> *O, could he but haue drawne his wit*
> *As well in brasse, as he hath hit*
> *His face; the Print would then surpasse*
> *All, that was euer writ in brasse.*
> *But, since he cannot, Reader, looke*
> *Not on his Picture, but his Booke.*[2]

The first four lines make a quiet opening, and the last two lines a quiet ending; but in between come four lines where the pace is more urgent and the movement more complex:

> *O, could he but haue drawne his wit*
> *As well in brasse, as he hath hit*
> *His face; the Print would then surpasse*
> *All, that was euer writ in brasse.*

The enjambement here gives the impression of strong feelings held under control. Also, the pauses made by the enjambement, and by the use of a periodic sentence, lead to a climax in the last line where 'All' comes with great force and emphasis, and 'that was euer writ in brasse'

---

1. Hollander, *op. cit.*, pp. 19–20.
2. Herford, VIII, 390.

is allowed to run out freely in contrast with the lines before.[1]

With the frequent contemporary references, the colloquial diction, and the colloquial rhythms, we find also references that are not contemporary, or at least not contemporary in the same obvious sense. For instance, no one can fail to be struck by the number of times Jonson mentions the myth of the Golden Age in his poems. It is not surprising that he does so, since this myth makes a fit symbol for his ideal of perfection. It comes naturally to him to describe the subject of a complimentary poem as 'thou piece of the first times'[2] or, at greater length and in more detail, to write thus to Benjamin Rudyerd:

> *If I would wish, for truth, and not for show,*
> *The aged Satvrne's age, and rites to know;*
> *If I would striue to bring backe times, and trie*
> *The world's pure gold, and wise simplicitie ...*
> *I need no other arts, but studie thee ...*[3]

or, to another subject of compliment:

> *Whil'st thou art certaine to thy words, once gone,*
> *As is thy conscience, which is alwayes one:*
> *The* Virgin, *long-since fled from earth, I see,*
> *T⟨o⟩'our times return'd, hath made her heauen in thee.*[4]

Even when this vision of past perfection is expressed in Christian terms, it is the same vision:

> *A forme more fresh, then are the* Eden *bowers,*
> *And lasting, as her flowers ...*[5]

---

1. Some of Wyatt's poems too have as their main attraction a subtle, and carefully controlled, use of syntax and verse-form to emphasize the meaning. Here, for instance, it is remarkable how much stress is laid on 'thrall':

> *Wherefore all ye*
> *That after shall*
> *Bye ffortune be,*
> *As I am, thrall,*
>
> *Example take ...*

(*Collected Poems of Sir Thomas Wyatt*, ed. Kenneth Muir, first published 1949, quoted from 1963 impression, Poem 157, p. 146.)

2. 'To Sir William Vvedale', Herford, VIII, 79.

3. 'To the same', *ibid.*, 78.

4. 'To Thomas Lord Chancelor ⟨Egerton⟩', *ibid.*, 52.

5. 'Epode', *ibid.*, 111.

It is the same vision of natural happiness, complete honesty, and perfect justice.

When Jonson wrote, the classical myths had long been naturalized in the minds of English readers of poetry, although Jonson had to make an effort to naturalize the gods of Greece and Rome in the landscape of the British Isles. The 'Ode. ἀλληγορικὴ',[1] for instance, shows, as G. B. Johnston says, 'a definite naturalizing of myth in the geography of Great Britain'.[2] The effort had to be made, but it was successful, and if, as Walton says, 'there was no impassable gap between the world of the poet's vision and Jacobean and Caroline England',[3] no writer did more than Jonson to close whatever gap there was. The worth of present-day reality was assessed in the light of ideals, not merely taken from the past (that would have made the dominant note one of nostalgia, which it certainly is not), but from myths which were, and still are, part of the literary consciousness of Europe:

> *Thus Pan, and Sylvane, hauing had their rites,*
> *Comvs puts in, for new delights;*
> *And fills thy open hall with mirth, and cheere,*
> *As if in Satvrne's raigne it were;*
> *Apollo's harpe, and Hermes lyre resound,*
> *Nor are the* Muses *strangers found:*
> *The rout of rurall folke come thronging in,*
> *(Their rudenesse then is thought no sinne)* . . .[4]

The last two lines here show how easily and naturally the idealized description of Sir Robert Wroth's household can come in a more down-to-earth description. Hussey makes an interesting contrast with Donne:

> Donne is so frequently autobiographical and writes as if he is still within the grasp of the experience. Jonson has long since assimilated the experience and places it in the light of a verdict from history before he writes.[5]

The poem to William, Earl of Newcastle also illustrates very well how

---

1. *Ibid.*, 366.
2. *Ben Jonson: Poet*, p. 39.
3. Walton, p. 44.
4. 'To Sir Robert Wroth', Herford, VIII, 98.
5. Maurice Hussey, Intr. to *Jonson and the Cavaliers* 1964, p. 12.

myth can be used as a means of elegant compliment:

> *When first, my Lord, I saw you backe your horse,*
> *Provoke his mettall, and command his force*
> *To all the uses of the field, and race,*
> *Me thought I read the ancient Art of* Thrace,
> *And saw a Centaure, past those tales of* Greece;
> *So seem'd your horse and you, both of a peece!*
> *You shew'd like* Perseus *upon* Pegasus;
> *Or* Castor *mounted on his* Cyllarus;
> *Or what we heare our home-borne Legend tell,*
> *Of bold Sir* Bevis, *and his* Arundell:
> *Nay, so your Seate his beauties did endorse,*
> *As I began to wish my selfe a horse.*[1]

The pun on 'endorse' leads naturally to the touch of humour in the last line which is in keeping with the rest of the poem where Jonson takes seriously, but not solemnly, 'those tales of *Greece*'.

 This use of myths and mythological figures to convey the abstract ideas they embody is sometimes called the allegorical use of myth. It is true that Christians were reconciled to the study of pagan literature and to a natural delight in the pagan pantheon by the method of allegorical explanation:

> Throughout the Middle Ages, and the Renaissance as well, Plato's objections to poetry were recurrently fortified by Christian objections to pagan and often immoral writings. These Platonic and patristic and 'puritan' complaints were met, during the Middle Ages and not seldom in the Renaissance, by the doctrine of allegorical truth contained beneath the husk of fiction. This allegorical and defensive method of exegesis, which had been practised in Greece before Plato, was later applied to both the Bible and the classics, notably the *Aeneid* and even the more doubtful poetry of Ovid; and it was given a popular restatement for the Renaissance by Boccaccio.[2]

Some idea of how far this allegorizing could go can be gained from Edgar Wind's *Pagan Mysteries in the Renaissance*. There are, for instance, the suggested reasons Wind quotes why the Graces should

---

1. Herford, VIII, 228.
2. Douglas Bush, *Classical Influences in Renaissance Literature*, p. 23.

be represented as naked: they had apparently once been clothed.[1]
This is interesting when we remember Jonson's line:

Truth, and the Graces best, when naked are.[2]

At the same time, I think it would be misleading to imply that great
learning was necessary to appreciate such references in a vernacular
poem. In the Renaissance the reader who found himself lost did not
have to search the classics:

Recent scholarship has revealed to what an unexpected – and yet
altogether natural – degree even learned writers of the Renaissance
made use of dictionaries of mythology, a practice that to some
people may carry a suggestion of the second-hand and cheap. But,
since all poets had some classical education and a feeling for
antiquity, it made small difference where an immediate hint came
from. And the importance of handbooks of myth, such as those of
Boccaccio and Natalis Comes and Cartari, was not merely that they
fulfilled the function of similar modern books, but still more that
they gave allegorical and ethical interpretations. It was no less
legitimate and fruitful, for such well-educated poets as Spenser and
Chapman and even the learned Jonson, to use such works than it
was for Mr Eliot to use *The Golden Bough.*[3]

A modern variant of such handbooks is Robert Graves's *The Greek
Myths*[4] in which the interpretations are not allegorical or ethical but,
in accordance more with modern interest and scholarship, anthropo-
logical. In brief, Jonson used classical myth in a manner that is quite
familiar from other poetry in English right up to the present day.
Poets still go without ostentation to the pagan myths to illustrate their
thought, partly because of the perennial attractiveness of these most
likable of all the gods and partly because of what they stand for or can
be made to stand for:

Helen being chosen found life flat and dull
And later had much trouble from a fool,
While that great Queen, that rose out of the spray,

---

1. Edgar Wind, *Pagan Mysteries in the Renaissance*, 1958, p. 34.
2. '*An Epistle to Master* Iohn Selden', Herford, VIII, 158.
3. Douglas Bush, *Classical Influences in Renaissance Literature*, p. 42. See also E. W.
Talbert, 'New Light on Ben Jonson's Workmanship', *S.P.*, XL (1943), 154–85.
4. In two vols., 1955.

> *Being fatherless could have her way*
> *Yet chose a bandy-leggèd smith for man.*
> *It's certain that fine women eat*
> *A crazy salad with their meat*
> *Whereby the Horn of Plenty is undone.*[1]

Another striking, and even more recent, instance of the expression of a contemporary sensibility through classical reference is Auden's 'The Shield of Achilles'[2] where Christian mysteries are glimpsed through pagan myth.

I think C. F. Wheeler is wrong in describing as 'confusion' the freedom with which Jonson handles his myths:

> In the many instances of Jonson's alluding to Cupid, or Eros, or Love, there is much confusion, for while at times he presents definitely mythological notions, at other times he seems to be meditating philosophically upon a subject which fascinated him. This observation is particularly true when he uses the word 'Love' as synonymous with Cupid...[3]

This:

> *...Cvpid, who (at first) tooke vaine delight,*
> *In meere out-formes, vntill he lost his sight,*
> *Hath chang'd his soule, and made his obiect you:*
> *Where finding so much beautie met with vertue,*
> *He hath not onely gain'd himselfe his eyes...*[4]

and this:

> *The thing, they here call Loue, is blinde Desire,*
> *Arm'd with bow, shafts, and fire...*[5]

are no more confused than this:

> *A Helen of social welfare dream,*
> *Climb on a wagonette to scream.*[6]

It is not 'confusion' we find in either Jonson or Yeats, but simply an

---

1. 'A Prayer for my Daughter', W. B. Yeats, *op. cit.*, p. 212.
2. *The Shield of Achilles*, 1955, p. 35.
3. *Classical Mythology in the Plays, Masques, and Poems of Ben Jonson*, 1938, p. 69.
4. 'To Mrs Philip Sydney', Herford, VIII, 73–4.
5. 'Epode', *ibid.*, 110.
6. 'Why should not Old Men be Mad?', W. B. Yeats, *op. cit.*, p. 388.

extension of the meaning inherent in the myth till it becomes a sort of metaphor, or till the distinction between reference and metaphor becomes one not worth making:

> *Some act of* Loue's *bound to reherse,*
> *I thought to binde him, in my verse:*
> *Which when he felt, Away (quoth hee)*
> *Can Poets hope to fetter mee?*
> *It is enough, they once did get*
> *Mars, and my* Mother, *in their net:*
> *I weare not these my wings in vaine.*
> *With which he fled me: and againe,*
> *Into my ri'mes could ne're be got*
> *By any arte. Then wonder not,*
> *That since, my numbers are so cold,*
> *When* Loue *is fled, and I grow old.*[1]

Classical allusions and references come easily to Jonson, whether in important comparisons:

> *Shee is* Venus, *when she smiles,*
> *But shee's* Juno, *when she walkes,*
> *And* Minerva, *when she talkes,*[2]

or in glancing references like this:

> *Yet should the Lover still be ayrie and light,*
> *In all his Actions rarified to spright;*
> *Not, like a* Midas, *shut up in himselfe,*
> *And turning all he toucheth into pelfe,*[3]

or this, a description of barristers:

> *Hook-handed* Harpies, *gowned Vultures . . .*[4]

or so much taken for granted that the myth is only faintly suggested:

> *To vrge, my lou'd Alphonso, that bold fame*
> *Of building townes, and making wilde beasts tame,*
> *Which* Musick *had . . .*[5]

---

1. 'Why I write not of Love', Herford, VIII, 93.
2. *'His discourse with* Cupid', *ibid.*, 137.
3. *'An Elegie', ibid.*, 197.
4. *'An Epigram to the Councellor that pleaded, and carried the Cause', ibid.*, 187.
5. 'To Alphonso Ferrabosco, *on his Booke', ibid.*, 82.

or:

> *Mixe then your Notes, that we may prove*
> *To stay the running floods,*
> *To make the Mountaine Quarries move,*
> *And call the walking woods.*[1]

This familiarity leads naturally to a playful use of myth, particularly suitable for lighthearted and urbane compliments:[2]

> *Retyr'd, with purpose your faire worth to praise,*
> *'Mongst Hampton shades, and Phoebvs groue of bayes,*
> *I pluck'd a branch; the iealous god did frowne,*
> *And bad me lay th'vsurped laurell downe:*
> *Said I wrong'd him, and (which was more) his loue.*
> *I answer'd, Daphne now no paine can proue.*
> *Phoebvs replyed. Bold head, it is not shee:*
> *Cary my loue is, Daphne but my tree.*[3]

This playful use of myth becomes even more sophisticated when Jonson rejects the pagan gods as unsuitable for his poetry at the same time as he is making poetry from them and their rejection:

> *And must I sing? what subiect shall I chuse?*
> *Or whose great name in* Poets *heauen vse,*
> *For the more countenance to my actiue* Muse?
>
> *Hercvles? alas his bones are yet sore,*
> *With his old earthly labours . . .*
>
> *Goe, crampe dull Mars, light Venvs, when he snorts,*
> *Or, with thy Tribade trine, inuent new sports,*
> *Thou, nor thy looseness with my making sorts.*[4]

---

1. '*The Musicall strife; In a Pastorall Dialogue*', ibid., 143.
2. As in '*An Epigram. To* William, *Earle of* Newcastle', *ibid.*, 228. Quoted above, p. 86.
3. 'To his Lady, then Mrs Cary', Herford, VIII, 80. Cf.:
> The Gods, *that mortal Beauty chase,*
> *Still in a Tree did end their race.*
> Apollo *hunted* Daphne *so,*
> *Only that She might Laurel grow.*
> *And* Pan *did after* Syrinx *speed,*
> *Not as a Nymph, but for a Reed.*

('The Garden', *The Poems and Letters of Andrew Marvell*, ed. H.M. Margoliouth, I, 1927, 48.)
4. 'And must I sing? . . .', Herford, VIII, 107.

The sophisticated and urbane tone which pervades Jonson's poetry is related by Geoffrey Walton to what he calls 'the old idea of courtesy'.[1] Walton writes:

His poetry, even more than his plays, links seventeenth-century culture and the polite civilization of the Augustans to the better features of the medieval social order and to the half-religious ideal of Courtesy.[2]

Discussing 'the prevailing urbane elegance' which he admires in the Caroline poets, F. R. Leavis, while recognizing the support it had from contemporary manners, stresses that it was also a poetic achievement for which Jonson was largely responsible:

. . . while this elegance has fairly obvious social correlations, it could not as a literary mode have been achieved by Carew (or any other of the Court group) if there had been no other major influence besides Donne's. For this influence the acclamation of the age itself leads us to Ben Jonson.[3]

Since poetry had, in Jonson's day, an important part to play in social life, it is not surprising that it was usually expected to be well-mannered: it is natural that an urbane society should demand that some at least of its poetry be urbane also, and any tendency which such a society may have to look sometimes for the expression of the opposite qualities – lack of restraint, even savagery – was amply catered for in Jonson's day by the stage. At the same time even the Court society of Jacobean and Caroline England was urbane by aspiration rather than in achievement, and it realized in its poetry ideals which were often ignored elsewhere. Certainly what we know of Jonson's life and manners does not prepare us for the tact and courtesy of his poetry. As a man he was outspoken to the point of rudeness, quarrelsome, and at times physically violent, all with a lusty enjoyment of his faults. We must simply be grateful that his poetry is not guilty of assault and battery, and we must recognize that poets, more than kings, may often be 'the makers of manners',[4] even of manners that seem to play little part in their own lives.

---

1. Walton, p. 27. Walton is speaking here of the poem 'High-spirited friend . . . ' Herford, VIII, 180.
2. Walton, p. 44.
3. Leavis, *op. cit.*, p. 17.
4. *King Henry V*, v. ii. 286–7, ed. J. H. Walter, 1954, p. 152.

When Jonson recommends in *Discoveries* that letter-writers should
use (as Ladies doe in their attyre) a diligent kind of negligence, and
their sportive freedome . . .[1]

he is also, possibly unintentionally but nevertheless almost inevitably,
characterizing one of the most pleasing features of his own poetry.
Very many of his poems are in fact letters, and they have the qualities
we look for in letters. In such poems urbanity is largely a matter of
suiting the tone to the complex relationship between the writer, the
recipient, and the subject matter. A tone of unbending solemnity
might achieve politeness, but not urbanity. The 'sportive freedome'
with which Jonson speaks to his readers is very attractive, and it must
have been even more attractive to those for whom the poems were
first written. It was a great achievement to tease a titled lady in a
manner that was stimulating without being too familiar:

> *You will not from the paper slightly passe:*
> *No lady, but, at some time, loues her glasse.*[2]

Even when Jonson is not writing a compliment, but asserting his
rights, he can still be urbane:

> *What can the cause be, when the* K⟨ing⟩ *hath given*
> *His* Poët *Sack, the* House-hold *will not pay?*
> *Are they so scanted in their store? or driven*
> *For want of knowing the* Poët, *to say him nay?*
> *Well, they should know him, would the* K⟨ing⟩ *but grant*
> *His* Poët *leave to sing his* House-hold *true;*
> *Hee'ld frame such ditties of their store, and want,*
> *Would make the very* Greene-cloth *to looke blew:*
> *And rather wish, in their expence of Sack,*
> *So, the allowance from the King to use,*
> *As the old* Bard, *should no Canary lack.*
> *'T were better spare a Butt, then spill his* Muse.[3]

Not only is Jonson's threat good-natured, without being too good-
natured to be taken seriously, but he disarmingly laughs at himself,
'the old *Bard*', while still insisting that as the King's poet he is worthy
of respect.

---

1. Herford, VIII, 632.
2. '*Epistle*. To Katherine, Lady Avbigny', *ibid.*, 117.
3. '*An Epigram, To the House-hold*', *ibid.*, 241.

If this urbanity was also in Jonson's conversation it is not so surprising as it may at first appear that Herrick should praise him particularly for his wit. It is clear that Herrick uses the word 'wit' in something like its modern sense when he says:

> *each Verse of thine*
> *Out-did the meate, out-did*
> *the frolick wine.*

> *My Ben*
> *Or come agen:*
> *Or send to us,*
> *Thy wits great over-plus;*[1]

Herrick was a good judge and we can trust him more readily than Herford and Simpson who say of the famous '*wit-combats*':[2]

> It was not, perhaps, necessary to be a Shakespeare to score momentary triumphs over the solid but slow-moving intellect of Ben.[3]

If we accept that wit can lie in the tone and placing of a remark, then there is no problem; but it is true that Jonson does not show in his poetry the brilliant inventiveness for which Donne is justly famous. Copious wit like this was not Jonson's forte:

> *Were they but Crownes of France, I cared not,*
> *For, most of these, their naturall Countreys rot*
> *I think possesseth, they come here to us,*
> *So pale, so lame, so leane, so ruinous;*
> *And howsoe'r French Kings most Christian be,*
> *Their Crownes are circumcis'd most Iewishly.*
> *Or were they Spanish Stamps, still travelling,*
> *That are become as Catholique as their King,*
> *Those unlickt beare-whelps, unfil'd pistolets*
> *That (more than Canon shot) availes or lets;*
> *Which negligently left unrounded, looke*
> *Like many angled figures, in the booke*

---

1. '*An Ode for him*', Herford, XI, 416.
2. Fuller, *The History of the Worthies of England*, Herford, XI, 510. Quoted above, p. 4.
3. Herford, I, 58.

> *Of some great Conjurer that would enforce*
> *Nature, as these doe justice, from her course . . .*[1]

Walton describes Jonson's wit accurately when he says:

> As an intellectual force it has a disciplinary and clarifying rather
> than a free-ranging and elaborating effect . . .[2]

It is the sort of wit which often lends itself to incisive denunciation:

> *I oft looke on false coyne, to know't from true:*
> *Not that I loue it, more, then I will you.*[3]

Or again:

> *Peace, Luxurie, thou art like one of those*
> *Who, being at sea, suppose,*
> *Because they moue, the continent doth so.*[4]

Jonson's attack on 'Captayne Hvngry' and his account of all the places
he says he has visited is most successful in the comic image which
deflates him at the end of this passage:

> *Giue them your seruices, and embassies*
> *In* Ireland, Holland, Sweden, *pompous lies,*
> *In* Hungary, *and* Poland, Turkie *too;*
> *What at* Ligorne, Rome, Florence *you did doe:*
> *And, in some yeere, all these together heap'd,*
> *For which there must more sea, and land be leap'd,*
> *If but to be beleeu'd you haue the hap,*
> *Then can a flea at twise skip i' the Map.*[5]

With the image of the flea on the map we move suddenly, and wittily,
from the exciting world of foreign travel and great affairs of state to
the English eating-house in which 'Captayne Hvngry' is merely
hungry.

---

1. 'ELEGIE XI. *The Bracelet*', Grierson, p. 97. Perhaps it was because it was in a style he
could not command that Jonson admired this poem so much: 'he esteemeth John Done
the first poet jn the World jn some things his verses of the Lost Chaine, he heth by Heart
& that passage of the calme, that dust and feathers doe not stirr, all was so quiet.
affirmeth Done to have written all his best pieces err he was 25 years old.' (*Conversations*,
Herford, I, 135).

2. Walton, p. 27.

3. 'To Captayne Hvngry', Herford, VIII, 68.

4. 'Epode', *ibid.*, 111.

5. *Ibid.*, 69.

Sometimes Jonson's wit takes the form of conscious hyperbole. This can be used for satiric effect:

> *...their very trade*
> *Is borrowing; that but stopt, they doe invade*
> *All as their prize, turne Pyrats here at Land,*
> *Ha' their* Bermudas, *and their streights i' th' Strand...*[1]

Sometimes he uses it for self-mockery:

> *I foole-hardie, there up-tooke*
> *Both the Arrow he had quit,*
> *And the Bow: with thought to hit*
> *This my object. But she threw*
> *Such a Lightning (as I drew)*
> *At my face, that tooke my sight,*
> *And my motion from me quite;*
> *So that, there, I stood a stone,*
> *Mock'd of all: and call'd of one*
> *(Which with griefe and wrath I heard)*
> Cupids *Statue with a Beard,*
> *Or else one that plaid his Ape,*
> *In a* Hercules-*his shape.*[2]

Passages like this are worth emphasizing, partly because Jonson's ability to laugh at himself is one of his most endearing characteristics and responsible for much of the charm of his writing, but more because they remind us how false is the common idea of him as a dull pedant with only the coarsest sense of humour. Coarse he certainly could be, but the humour in lines like these is delicate and restrained.

Often the self-mockery is less obvious, particularly when it does not involve hyperbole:

> *...he dares, at dice,*
> *Blaspheme god, greatly. Or some poore hinde beat,*
> *That breathes in his dogs way: and this is great.*
> *Nay more, for greatnesse sake, he will be one,*
> *May heare my* Epigrammes, *but like of none.*[3]

---

1. 'An Epistle to Sir Edward Sacvile, now Earle of Dorset', *ibid.*, 155.
2. '*How he saw her*', *ibid.*, 132.
3. 'On Don Svrly', *ibid.*, 36.

Surely Jonson is mocking himself as well as 'Don Svrly' in those last two lines? If it seems unlikely that he would mock anything so important as his own writing, then it is worth remembering this passage from *Discoveries*, his advice to a poet whose work does not at first succeed:

> ... try an other time, with labour. If then it succeed not, cast not away the Quills, yet: nor scratch the Wainescott, beate not the poore Deske; but bring all to the forge, and file, againe; tourne it a newe. There is no Statute *Law* of the Kingdome bidds you bee a Poet, against your will; or the first Quarter.[1]

In his self-mockery, however, Jonson usually concentrates on his own body, and then we may reasonably presume he is using hyperbole:

> *Why? though I seeme of a prodigious wast,*
> *I am not so voluminous, and vast,*
> *But there are lines, wherewith I might b⟨e⟩'embrac'd.*
>
> *'Tis true, as my wombe swells, so my backe stoupes,*
> *And the whole lumpe growes round, deform'd, and droupes,*
> *But yet the Tun at Heidelberg had houpes.*
>
> *You were not tied, by any Painters Law,*
> *To square my Circle, I confesse; but draw*
> *My Superficies: that was all you saw.*
>
> *Which if in compasse of no Art it came*
> *To be describ'd ⟨but⟩ by a Monogram,*
> *With one great blot, yo' had form'd me as I am.*[2]

And he mocks himself in this poem as a preliminary to insisting, as he so often does, on the power of poetry to pierce below the surface of things and glorify 'the beauties of the mind':[3]

> *But, you are he can paint; I can but write:*
> *A Poet hath no more but black and white,*
> *Ne knowes he flatt'ring Colours, or false light.*

---

1. *Ibid.*, 637–8.
2. '*My Answer. The Poet to the Painter*', ibid., 226–7.
3. '*Epistle.* To Katherine, Lady Avbigny', *ibid.*, 117.

Yet when of friendship I would draw the face,
A letter'd mind, and a large heart would place
To all posteritie; I will write Burlase.[1]

---

1. '*My Answer. The Poet to the Painter*', *ibid.*, 227.

3
'Things Manly, and not Smelling Parasite'[1]

I have deliberately avoided any attempt to place Jonson's poems into rigidly defined categories, either by using what might seem to be the convenient divisions suggested by the volumes into which his work is divided or by recourse to the Renaissance doctrine of kinds. Only two volumes, *Epigrammes* and *The Forrest*, were prepared and edited completely by Jonson himself; *Underwoods* was published after his death, and how far he would have approved of its contents or their arrangement is uncertain; the last group, which Herford and Simpson call *Ungathered Verse*, consists overtly of miscellaneous pieces and cannot even pretend to any particular arrangement.[2] Then, even the volume of *Epigrammes*, of which Jonson was so proud, contains such variety and has such little pretence to necessary order that Herford and Simpson refer to it as 'a quite unmanageable wilderness of verse-kinds';[3] one poem in it, 'On the famovs Voyage',[4] cannot by any stretch of the imagination be called an epigram. As for dividing the poems by kinds – Jonson mixes the kinds so much that the doctrine, if it does not break down, at least has to admit so many sub-divisions and mixed kinds that it is of no use for my purpose. Few of his eulogies are without incidental satire or invective, and his elegies naturally modulate into eulogy and also usually contain satire or invective; even his lyrics contain much variety.

Moreover, it is not helpful to consider Jonson's poems in order of composition, even when this is known, for there is no sense of a gradual development either of attitude or style.[5] His best poems are to be found scattered throughout the different collections.

I propose then, in this chapter, to consider in some detail a selection of Jonson's best 'occasional' poetry, and leave his lyrics for separate treatment. I wish to show in more detail how those features, of matter

---

1. 'To my Mvse', Herford, VIII, 48.
2. Herford, II, 337; G. B. Johnston, *Ben Jonson: Poet*, p. 14.
3. Herford, II, 341.
4. Herford, VIII, 84.
5. Herford, I, 120: '. . . of the extraordinary power of inner growth, which astonishes us in a Dante, a Shakespeare, a Goethe, there is little trace in Jonson.'

and of style, which were mentioned in the first two chapters, are revealed in the larger context of whole poems.

There are, of course, many poems by Jonson which, while they may not have been suggested by any particular occasion, read as though they were. One such is '*An Elegie*', 'Since you must goe, and I must bid farewell'.[1] It is a love-poem, and indirectly a eulogy of the mistress, but as so often with Jonson the eulogy is made from something like mockery; the net result is not the expression of passion so much as the probing of a psychological state.

The poem opens, typically, with lines that have all the appearance of speech:

> *Since you must goe, and I must bid farewell,*
> *Heare, Mistris, your departing servant tell*
> *What it is like . . .*

Also typically, the mistress is soon advised to sit up and take notice of what is being said and understand it correctly:

> *And doe not thinke they can*
> *Be idle words, though of a parting Man.*

By using the word 'servant' Jonson has already suggested that he is writing within the convention of Courtly Love, and the description of himself as her 'Man' underlines this.[2]

Having established the right convention for his poem, Jonson goes on to develop ideas natural to this convention; but, as so often with him, he develops them with his own slant. There is the hyperbolic expression of the darkness of life without the mistress:

> *It is as if a night should shade noone-day,*
> *Or that the Sun was here, but forc't away;*
> *And we were left under that Hemisphere,*
> *Where we must feele it Darke for halfe a yeare.*

Then Jonson affects to take his own figurative expressions literally:

> *What fate is this, to change mens dayes and houres,*
> *To shift their seasons, and destroy their powers!*

---

1. Herford, VIII, 199.
2. I think 'Man' does mean 'servant' here, since there is no reason why anyone should expect 'idle' words at parting (in fact just the opposite), while it was presumably usual to take small notice of what the servants said.

The effect is not to ridicule the conventional and hyperbolic manner of expression, but to use it while showing an awareness that the attitude it expresses is at least somewhat exaggerated. To call this, or the following lines, satire on Courtly Love, would be to miss the delicate balance that is maintained:

> *Alas I ha' lost my heat, my blood, my prime,*
> *Winter is come a Quarter e're his Time,*
> *My health will leave me; and when you depart,*
> *How shall I doe, sweet Mistris, for my heart?*

In this convention, hearts were accustomed to travelling from one body into another, and Jonson plays witty variations on this notion simply by following through some of the consequences of it:

> *You would restore it? No, that's worth a feare,*
> *As if it were not worthy to be there:*
> *O, keepe it still; for it had rather be*
> *Your sacrifice, then here remaine with me.*

With just a touch of mockery, he adds 'And so I spare it', and then, since without a heart he must be dead, finishes by saying in delicate self-mockery:

> *Come what can become*
> *Of me, I'le softly tread unto my Tombe;*
> *Or like a Ghost walke silent amongst men,*
> *Till I may see both it and you agen.*

The total effect of this poem is not easy to define. Adoration is there, but expressed with an awareness that other feelings are possible; the poet sees his own situation (whether real or imagined does not matter) in a wider context where it is only one of a number of ways of feeling. The poem is a compliment to the lady, a compliment not only to her ability to inspire adoration but also to her understanding and sensibility: it implies that she will be able to appreciate urbanity and wit.

The term 'occasional' is one that might be applied to almost all Jonson's poems, from, say, the eulogies on Lucy, Countess of Bedford,[1] to the attack 'On Gvt'.[2] 'On Gvt' may or may not have been

---

1. Herford, VIII, 52, 54, 60, 662.
2. *Ibid.*, 76.

inspired by a real person, but – like most of Jonson's poems – it reads as though it were. His poems are public performances, speaking with authority on matters of public concern, and not self-communings of the poet which the reader is privileged to overhear.[1] Indeed much of the variety of his poetry is due to the variety of people whom he knew[2] – writers, musicians, aristocrats, and 'Car-men'.[3] As Herford and Simpson stress,[4] his epistles read as though they were addressed to individuals and their tone varies according to the individual addressed, even though they are also public performances.

The title *Epigrammes* can be misleading. If we expect 'jewels five-words long',[5] we are disappointed. For all his gift for the terse phrase, Jonson is not usually at his best in his short pieces.[6] His poems need space to gather momentum, and his most powerful phrases gain much of their strength from their context. There are exceptions, of course, poems which are both short and successful:

On Banck the Vsvrer

Banck feeles no lamenesse of his knottie gout,
His monyes trauaile for him, in and out:
And though the soundest legs goe euery day,
He toyles to be at hell, as soone as they.[7]

This has the element of surprise which is so effective in satirical epi-gram, a sensuous force in the phrase 'knottie gout',[8] an apposite concentration of meaning in 'trauaile' (travail and travel), an impli-cation in 'the soundest legs' that Banck is unsound morally as well as physically, and the true harsh satiric laughter in 'toyles to be at hell'.

However, Jonson is usually at his best when there is more space to fight in. The poem 'The new Crie'[9] has more than once been praised

---

1. In his awareness of his audience, Jonson is a typical Renaissance poet. See Tuve, p. 180.
2. F. W. Bradbrook, *op. cit.*, pp. 131–2.
3. 'The Voyage it selfe', Herford, VIII, 86.
4. Herford, II, 338.
5. Tennyson, 'The Princess; A Medley', *Poetical Works* (Oxford Standard Authors), 1953, reprinted 1959, p. 166.
6. Herford, II, 356.
7. Herford, VIII, 36.
8. Admittedly an exact translation of Horace's 'nodosa cheragra'. See Herford, XI, 7.
9. Herford, VIII, 58. For this, and for other poems of any length discussed in this chapter, I include line-numbers under the quotations.

and compared to Dryden.[1] The comparison is a just one, for the prevailing attitude in the poem to its victims, those who pride themselves on their knowledge of secret state affairs, is one of contempt. Also, as is normal in Dryden but rare in Jonson, the poem manages to stay this side of anger, and the restraint adds force:

> *They carry in their pockets Tacitvs,*
> *And the Gazetti, or Gallo-Belgicvs:*
> *And talke reseru'd, lock'd vp, and full of feare,*
> *Nay, aske you, how the day goes, in your eare.*
> *Keepe a* starre-*chamber sentence close, twelue dayes:*
> *And whisper what a Proclamation sayes.*
> (15–20)

The ebullient opening, so clearly and firmly set in the London of Jonson's day,

> *Ere cherries ripe, and strawberries be gone,*
> *Vnto the cryes of* London *Ile adde one;*
> *Ripe statesmen, ripe: They grow in euery street.*
> *At sixe and twentie, ripe. You shall 'hem meet,*
> (1–4)

modulates into an apparently serious consideration of the 'statesmen' which is only a blind for a sudden satirical twist:

> *Yet haue they seene the maps, and bought 'hem too,*
> *And vnderstand ' hem, as most chapmen doe.*
> (9–10)

The poem continues, through a typical group of local and topical references, to a typical definition of the terms used in the poem:

> *And therefore doe not onely shunne*
> *Others more modest, but contemne vs too,*
> *That know not so much state, wrong, as they doo.*
> (38–40)

This poem does, it is true, illustrate one hindrance to an appreciation of Jonson: it is topical in a rather damaging way; even with annotation, the full force of, say, '*Porta*'[2] is hard to recapture. Also, the

---

1. Castelain, p. 771; Swinburne, p. 96.
2. Line 25.

progressions to contempt are often coarser than with Dryden, as here
up to 'pisse':

> *They 'haue found the sleight*
> *With iuyce of limons, onions, pisse, to write . . .*
>
> (27–8)

Nevertheless, the poem as a whole reveals an energy and accumulation
of satiric detail which is most pleasing.

According to Herford and Simpson, 'An Expostulaĉon wᵗʰ Inigo
Iones'[1]

> gains little by the free rein which Jonson has given to his rancour.
> Even as a piece of invective it fatally lacks sinew, while its force as
> argument is impaired by the blind and futile cavils which mingle
> with the just charges, involving the architect of genius in the same
> anathema as the too-ambitious stage-manager who took 'painting
> and carpentry' to be 'the soul of Masque' . . .[2]

I do not agree with the implication there that invective is an inferior
kind of poetry. Moreover, I think one of the merits of the 'Expostulaĉon' is its muscularity, the sheer strength of its sustained and varied
attack, which makes up for its lack of subtlety, as here with its typical
contrast between appearance and reality:

> *your Trappings will not change you. Change yoʳ mynd.*
> *Noe veluet Sheath you weare, will alter kynde.*
> *A wodden Dagger, is a Dagger of wood*
> *Though gold or Iuory haftes would make it good.*
>
> (25–8)

This contrast is at the centre of the poem, which is much more than
an attack by Ben Jonson on his arch-enemy Inigo Jones: it is honesty
complaining of dishonesty, simplicity of pretentiousness, and poetry
asserting its predominance over all the other arts:[3]

> *Oh, to make Boardes to speake ! There is a taske*
> *Painting & Carpentry are yᵉ Soule of Masque.*

---

1. Herford, VIII, 402.
2. Herford, II, 357.
3. Trimpi, p. 160: 'The competition between Jones and Jonson was fundamentally one
between painting, which spoke to the sense, and poetry, which spoke to the understanding.
Their rivalry can be described, by analogy, as one between rhetoric and dialectic, between
a rhetorical and a plain style. The analogy is helpful, for it explains how Jonson's passionate
anger against Jones arose, in part at least, from his convictions about art in general and
literature in particular.'

Pack w^{t}h your pedling Poetry to the Stage,
This is ye money-gett, Mechanick Age!
To plant ye Musick where noe eare can reach!
Attyre ye Persons as noe thought can teach
Sense, what they are!

(49–55)

It is because the poem is generalized as well as very personal in its attack that I think Herford and Simpson's second criticism, that the poem is unfair to the ability of Jones, is on dubious ground. Literary attacks are often unfair: Dryden was arguably unfair to Shadwell,[1] and most of us hope that Swift was unfair to the human race in the fourth book of *Gulliver's Travels*. The main question is whether the attack is consistent and convincing in itself, whatever its fairness in relation to our knowledge outside the poem. There is, admittedly, a real difficulty here, and one which we often meet in Jonson's poetry. The difficulty is increased for me since I have already argued that Jonson's poems often gain in effectiveness when read in a wide context;[2] and it would not seem fair here simply to abstract this poem from everything else we know about Inigo Jones. Nevertheless, I think the poem is successful, and I suggest that the most immediate context for it is made by all the other poems Jonson devoted to Jones, and that Jones is made into a sort of legendary buffoon by Jonson. We have to make some distinction between Jones as he really was, in so far as we can know that, and the 'Asinigo'[3] which is largely a creation by Jonson:

His 'speculum consuetudinis' was a kind of magic mirror which slightly distorted the objects it showed, thus heightening their deformity and making more obvious to the spectator their normal proportions.[4]

Moreover, to see the poem simply as an attack is to oversimplify it. Some lines are indeed very biting:

Controll Ctesibius: ouerbearing vs
With mistook Names out of Vitruvius!

(7–8)

---

1. 'Mac Flecknoe', *op. cit.*, p. 265.
2. See p. 12 above.
3. Line 20.
4. E. C. Dunn, *op. cit.*, p. xiii.

but others show a good humour which includes a few digs (gentle ones) at the writer himself:

> *I am too fat t'enuy him. He too leane*
> *To be worth Enuy. Henceforth I doe meane*
> *To pitty him...*
>
> (69–71)

Of course, 'fat' and 'leane' are meant partly in the sense of 'well-supplied' and 'ill-provided' (both with particular reference to artistic ability); but their more obvious physical meanings are there too. Jonson often laughed at his own corpulence. Also

> *Henceforth I doe meane*
> *To pitty him*

cannot be taken as an attempt to convey contempt, but rather as an expression of the wish to convey contempt, which is a very different thing. My main impression of the poem is that Jonson enjoyed writing it: a suitable epigraph would be:

> On an occasion of this kind it becomes more than a moral duty to speak one's mind. It becomes a pleasure.[1]

Such is the boisterous enjoyment which comes through that we even sense Jonson getting pleasure out of the technical devices he is attacking:

> *Henceforth I doe meane*
> *To pitty him, as smiling at his ffeat*
> *Of Lanterne-lerry: w^{t}h fuliginous heat*
> *Whirling his Whymseys, by a subtilty*
> *Suckt from ye Veynes of shop-philosophy...*
> *But wisest Inigo! who can reflect*
> *On ye new priming of thy old Signe postes*
> *Reuiuing w^{t}h fresh coulors ye pale Ghosts*
> *Of thy dead Standards: or (w^{t}h miracle) see*
> *Thy twice conceyud, thrice payd for Imagery?*
>
> (70–4, 86–90)

Herford and Simpson are even less appreciative of the poem 'On

---

1. Oscar Wilde, *The Importance of Being Earnest*, Act II, in *Plays, Prose Writings, and Poems*, Everyman's Library, 1930 and reprinted 1945, p. 383.

the famovs Voyage'[1] which Jonson included incongruously in his *Epigrammes* and which would perhaps be incongruous anywhere. They describe it as 'a boisterous freak of stercoraceous humour',[2] 'a bad joke',[3] and a 'hideous and unsavoury burlesque'.[4] Other critics agree. Johnston says it is 'perhaps the coarsest and most unsavoury of all his poems',[5] and Gregory Smith says that here Jonson 'dipped his quill in sewage'.[6] Swinburne does leave the hope that the poem may help Jonson's reputation abroad:

> ... all English readers, I trust, will agree with me that coprology should be left to Frenchmen ... It is nothing less than lamentable that so great an English writer as Ben Jonson should ever have taken the plunge of a Parisian diver into the cesspool...[7]

Unfortunately even a Frenchman is effronted:

> Ce morceau répugnant marque chez notre poète un goût fâcheux pour la scatologie; il nous prouve que son classicisme n'excluait pas certaine grossièreté rabelaisienne, qui n'est pas sauvée dans l'espèce par le bonheur de l'expression.[8]
>
> (This repugnant piece shows that our poet had an unfortunate taste for scatology; it proves to us that his classicism did not exclude a certain Rabelaisian coarseness, not excused in the case in point by the felicity of the expression.)

The poem certainly has a distinctive atmosphere, all 'the reek of the human' which Donald Davie looks for in great poetry.[9] The harsh criticisms I have quoted imply that there are some subjects with which poetry should not deal. This is a very difficult position to maintain. At the same time, poetry – and particularly public and occasional poetry – must take account of the manners and decorum in vogue outside the poem. Contemporaries must have found the subject matter of 'On the famovs Voyage' rather objectionable – otherwise

---

1. Herford, VIII, 84.
2. Herford, I, 63.
3. Herford, II, 341.
4. *Ibid.*, 339.
5. *Poems of Ben Jonson*, p. xlii.
6. Smith, p. 239.
7. Swinburne, p. 95.
8. Castelain, p. 765 (footnote).
9. *Articulate Energy*, 1955, p. 165.

there would have been no point in the joke: but they were less easily offended in this way than we are. Robert Lynd provides a clue, although he has not this poem in mind:

Probably improved sanitation has had more influence on literary manners than anyone yet suspects.[1]

The last two lines of the poem have for us an extra joke of which Jonson could not have been aware:

And I could wish for their eterniz'd sakes,
My Muse had plough'd with his, that sung A-iax.
(195–6)

In punning on the title of the book which describes the first flush-toilet,[2] Jonson reminds us of the invention which, more than anything else, makes his poem hard to take nowadays, for when we read it we

Must trie the 'vn-vsed valour of a nose.
(132)

It is interesting to see how the same difficulty arises with Auden's recent poem 'The Geography of the House':

Freud did not invent the
Constipated miser:
Banks have letter boxes
Built in their façade,
Marked For Night Deposits,
Stocks are firm or liquid,
Currencies of nations
Either soft or hard.[3]

This is reminiscent of:

In memorie of which most liquid deed,
The citie since hath rais'd a Pyramide.
(193–4)

If we can accept the subject matter of the poem, and its many

---

1. 'The Bounds of Decency' (1927), *Books and Writers*, 1952, p. 212.

2. Sir John Harington, *A New Discourse of a Stale Subject Called the Metamorphosis of Ajax*, ed. E. S. Donno, 1962. Harington's book was first published in 1596.

3. *About the House*, 1966, p. 27.

passages of sensuous description (for this poem of Jonson's is as sensuous as anyone could wish), then we shall find that 'le bonheur de l'expression' of which Castelain speaks[1] makes it a very good poem indeed. It is primarily a joke, and no less acceptable as a poem for that; but, like all the best jokes, it has its serious aspects. If we use Gilbert Highet's distinction between 'mock-heroic, where the treatment is grandiose; and burlesque, where the treatment is low',[2] then this poem is best described as a mixture of mock-heroic and burlesque with incidental contemporary satire.

The mock-heroic note runs throughout, since it is a voyage through a sewer which is being described in epic terms:

> *No more let* Greece *her bolder fables tell*
> *Of Hercvles, or Thesevs going to* hell,
> *Orphevs, Vlysses: or the* Latine Muse,
> *With tales of* Troyes *iust knight, our faiths abuse:*
> *We haue a Shelton, and a Heyden got,*
> *Had power to act, what they to faine had not.*
> (1–6)

In the best epic tradition, Jonson states his subject near the beginning:

> *I sing the braue aduenture of two wights,*
> (21)

and occasionally, as though he were a bard singing in a hall, recalls his audience's attention to the matter in hand:

> *Now, lordings, listen well.*
> (28)

and

> *A harder tasque, then either his to* Bristo',
> *Or his to* Antwerpe. *Therefore, once more, list ho'.*
> (39–40)

There, as elsewhere,[3] comic feminine rhyming assists the mock-heroic effect.[4] At times the mock-heroic note verges on the heroic:

---

1. Castelain, p. 765. Quoted above, p. 106.
2. *The Anatomy of Satire*, p. 106.
3. E.g. lines 35–6, 61–2, 77–8, 95–6, 189–90.
4. G.B. Johnston, *Poems of Ben Jonson*, p. xxxviii: '. . . the comical feminine rhymes in certain poems, notably "The Famous Voyage", foreshadowed the practice of Butler, Byron, Browning, and Gilbert.'

> Gorgonian *scolds, and* Harpyes: *on the other*
> *Hung stench, diseases, and old filth, their mother,*
>
> (69–70)

and indeed the voyage did have a touch of heroism about it.

The burlesque note is most evident in Jonson's mockery of the 'Machinery'[1] so necessary to an epic poem:

> *Alcides, be thou succouring to my song.*
> *Thou hast seene* hell (*some say*) *and know'st all nookes there,*
> *Canst tell me best, how euery* Furie *lookes there,*
> *And art a* god, *if* Fame *thee not abuses,*
> *Alwayes at hand, to aide the merry* Muses.
> *Great* Club-fist, *though thy backe, and bones be sore,*
> *Still, with thy former labours; yet, once more,*
> *Act a braue worke, call it thy last aduentry:*
> *But hold my torch, while I describe the entry*
> *To this dire passage. Say, thou stop thy nose:*
> '*Tis but light paines: Indeede this Dock's no rose.*
>
> (50–60)

Of course Hercules is being mocked here, but not only Hercules: Jonson's main target is those who insist on dragging the gods and heroes into everything they write. This is important for, while mock-heroic (speaking of Shelton and Heyden in terms usually reserved for Hercules, Theseus, Orpheus, Ulysses, or Aeneas) is clearly a method open to development (as Dryden and Pope were to show later), burlesque (speaking of Hercules as 'Great *Club-fist*') seems much more limited: we expect the joke to wear thin very quickly. Yet here Jonson's burlesque does more than merely add a little variety to a mock-heroic work.[2] So does his burlesque treatment of Mercury later in the poem. This is not simply degradation of Mercury for the sake of an easy laugh: it is also the means by which

---

1. Pope, Dedication to 'The Rape of the Lock': 'The *Machinery*, Madam, is a Term invented by the Criticks, to signify that Part which the Deities, Angels, or Dæmons, are made to act in a Poem: For the ancient Poets are in one respect like many modern Ladies; Let an Action be never so trivial in it self, they always make it appear of the utmost Importance.' *Op. cit.*, p. 217.

2. Geoffrey Tillotson, *Alexander Pope, The Rape of the Lock and other Poems*, 1940, third edition 1962, p. 108: '. . . though burlesque is inferior as a single method, it is found handy as a complication of mock-heroic.' Tillotson's distinction between mock-heroic and burlesque (*ibid.*, pp. 106–8) is of great interest.

Jonson satirizes contemporary quack remedies and those who offer them:

> *At this a loud*
> *Crack did report it selfe, as if a cloud*
> *Had burst with storme, and down fell, ab excelsis,*
> *Poore Mercvry, crying out on Paracelsvs,*
> *And all his followers, that had so abvs'd him:*
> *And, in so shitten sort, so long had vs'd him:*
> *For (where he was the god of eloquence,*
> *And subtiltie of mettalls) they dispense*
> *His spirits, now, in pills, and eeke in potions,*
> *Suppositories, cataplasmes, and lotions.*
> (93–102)

Other touches of satire are: the mention of 'the graue fart, late let in parliament'[1] which, whatever its immediate reference,[2] has the force of epigram and is applicable to many proceedings in that assembly; and the terse parenthesis on 'the beadle' which expresses neatly the annoyance felt at petty officialdom:

> *One said, it was bold Briarevs, or the beadle,*
> *(Who hath the hundred hands when he doth meddle)...*
> (81–2)

Most striking of all perhaps, as we should expect from Jonson and in a poem of this nature, is the satire on literary pretentiousness:

> *...me thinkes 'tis od,*
> *That all this while I haue forgot some god,*
> *Or goddesse to inuoke, to stuffe my verse;*
> *And with both bombard-stile, and phrase, rehearse*
> *The many perills of this Port, and how*
> *Sans helpe of Sybil, or a golden bough,*
> *Or magick sacrifice, they past along!*
> (43–9)

There again, the last three lines would, out of context, easily be taken for lines from a straight epic: the laughter involves love of what is laughed at.

---

1. Line 108.
2. See note in Herford, x, 74, on *Alchemist* II. ii. 63.

I hope I have said enough to show that the poem is worthy of serious consideration,[1] that it is remarkable for its energy and inventiveness and its creation of a world which, while it is certainly Jacobean London with its 'out-cryes of the damned in the *Fleet*'[2] and its 'loud Sepvlchres with their hourely knells',[3] is also a truly comic world of the imagination. That the poem is well-written can hardly be denied; we need, however, as C. S. Lewis has said of some of Dunbar's poems,

> to make a readjustment. We must sever the modern association which connects extreme indecency with technical coarseness of form and low social rank, and must think ourselves back into a world where great professional poets, for the entertainment of great lords and ladies, lavished their skill on humours now confined to the preparatory school or the barrack-room.[4]

Critics have been kinder to '*An Execration upon* Vulcan'[5] which is in many ways similar to 'On the famovs Voyage', and it is not hard to see why. The subject has nothing unpleasant about it, and there is an irresistible charm in a poem which shows a man laughing at the great misfortune of his house burning down. In fact, the combination of circumstances is so striking and appealing, that it is a wonder no one has suggested that Jonson might first have written the poem and then set fire to his house.

It is true that the poem calls for heavy annotation,[6] but it is worth studying with great attention. Herford and Simpson go so far as to say:

> The 'Execration upon Vulcan', which so pleasantly simulates satiric invective, hardly has its match in the verse of serio-comic bravery.[7]

Like 'On the famovs Voyage', the '*Execration*' is most obviously first an imaginative and well-sustained joke: it is so funny that even

1. Herford, II, 341: 'We need not consider the "Famous Voyage"...'
2. Line 172.
3. Line 174.
4. *English Literature in the Sixteenth Century Excluding Drama*, Volume III of *The Oxford History of English Literature*, 1954, quoted from reprint of 1962, p. 94.
5. Herford, VIII, 202.
6. Castelain, pp. 792–3.
7. Herford, II, 357.

Gregory Smith detects a 'streak of burlesque'[1] in it. It opens with a witty attack on Vulcan and his relatives:

> And why to me this, thou lame Lord of fire,
>> What had I done that might call on thine ire?
> Or urge thy Greedie flame, thus to devoure
>> So many my Yeares-labours in an houre?
> I ne'er attempted, Vulcan, 'gainst thy life;
>> Nor made least line of love to thy loose Wife;
> Or in remembrance of thy afront, and scorne,
>> With Clownes, and Tradesmen, kept thee clos'd in horne.
> 'Twas Jupiter that hurl'd thee headlong downe,
>> And Mars, that gave thee a Lanthorne for a Crowne.
> Was it because thou wert of old denied
>> By Jove to have Minerva for thy Bride,
> That since thou tak'st all envious care and paine,
>> To ruine any issue of the braine?
>
> (1–14)

Most of the jokes here are common ones: it is their cumulative effect, and the evidence they give of a loving study of the victim, which make the scolding so humorous. The attack is maintained throughout the poem, spreading at times to people outside Vulcan's circle of acquaintances, and it comes to a climax in the 'civill curse'[2] which concludes the poem.

As in 'On the famovs Voyage', Jonson's burlesque has a purpose beyond the mere humorous degradation of a famous figure. The attack on Vulcan is what holds together a remarkable variety of other victims – 'The learned Librarie of *Don Quixote*',[3] 'hard trifles'[4] giving more evidence of a poet's ingenuity than of his imagination, and contemporary journalism,[5] to mention only a few that are treated in some detail. Some of the best strokes of satire come in incidental remarks whose unexpectedness gives most of their force, as when Jonson mentions as among his books which were destroyed

---

1. Smith, p. 240.
2. Line 190.
3. Line 31.
4. Line 35.
5. Lines 77–82.

> *a Grammar too,*
> *To teach some that, their Nurses could ⟨not⟩ doe,*
> *The puritie of Language;*
>
> (91–3)

or as when, towards the end, the poem seems to become serious and then suddenly slides back into satire on 'most of the *Kings men*' and thence back to scolding:

> *We aske your absence here, we all love peace,*
> *And pray the fruites thereof, and the increase;*
> *So doth the* King, *and most of the* Kings men
> *That have good places: therefore once agen,*
> *Pox on thee,* Vulcan, *thy* Pandora's *pox,*
> *And all the Evils that flew out of her box*
> *Light on thee: Or if those plagues will not doo,*
> *Thy Wives pox on thee, and* B⟨ess⟩ B⟨roughton⟩s *too.*
>
> (209–16)

As in 'On the famovs Voyage', Jonson often shows a certain sympathy with what he is attacking, by the way he describes it:

> *The whole summe*
> *Of errant Knight-hood, with the ⟨ir⟩ Dames, and Dwarfes,*
> *The ⟨ir⟩ charmed Boates, and the ⟨ir⟩ inchanted Wharfes;*
> *The* Tristrams, Lanc'lots, Turpins, *and the* Peers,
> *All the madde* Rolands, *and sweet* Oliveers;
> *To* Merlins *Marvailes, and his* Caballs *losse,*
> *With the Chimaera of the* Rosie-Crosse,
> *Their Seales, their Characters, Hermetique rings,*
> *Their Jemme of Riches, and bright Stone, that brings*
> *Invisibilitie, and strength, and tongues . . .*
>
> (66–75)

It is not difficult in this poem to find lines containing shrewd comment with a significance much wider than the immediate context. An instance is the reference to his 'humble Gleanings in Divinitie'[1] lost in the fire, a reference which neatly expresses the intellectual dangers of religious controversy; his own notes were made

---

1. Line 102.

> *After the Fathers, and those wiser Guides*
> *Whom Faction had not drawne to studie sides.*
> (103–4)

Nevertheless, the effect of the poem can only be felt as a whole. The sustaining of the theme, and the inclusion of so much diverse matter in a homogeneous whole, constitute the main merit of the poem. No quotation can give an impression of the overall effect, but I shall quote one passage at length, the comment on the destruction of the Globe Theatre, to suggest the complexity of meaning and the variety of mood which lie beneath the simple expression:

> *See the worlds Ruines! nothing but the piles*
> *Left! and wit since to cover it with Tiles.*
> *The Brethren, they streight nois'd it out for Newes,*
> *'Twas verily some Relique of the Stewes:*
> *And this a Sparkle of that fire let loose*
> *That was rak'd up in the* Winchestrian *Goose*
> *Bred on the Banck, in time of Poperie,*
> *When* Venus *there maintain'd the Misterie.*
> *But, others fell with that conceipt by the eares,*
> *And cry'd, it was a threatening to the beares;*
> *And that accursed ground, the* Parish-Garden:
> *Nay, sigh'd a Sister, 'twas the Nun,* Kate Arden,
> *Kindled the fire! But then, did one returne,*
> *No foole would his owne harvest spoile, or burne!*
> *If that were so, thou rather would'st advance*
> *The place, that was thy Wives inheritance.*
> *O no, cry'd all,* Fortune, *for being a whore,*
> *Scap'd not his Justice any jot the more:*
> *He burnt that Idoll of the* Revels *too:*
> *Nay, let* White-Hall *with Revels have to doe,*
> *Though but in daunces, it shall know his power;*
> *There was a Judgement shew'n too in an houre.*
> *Hee is true* Vulcan *still! He did not spare*
> Troy, *though it were so much his* Venus *care.*
> *Foole, wilt thou let that in example come?*
> *Did she not save from thence, to build a* Rome?
> *And what hast thou done in these pettie spights,*
> *More then advanc'd the houses, and their rites?*

> *I will not argue thee, from those, of guilt,*
> *For they were burnt, but to be better built.*

(137–66)

Starting with a eulogistic pun on the name of the Globe and a gentle dig at the lack of foresight of its first builders, this passage proceeds with a continuation of the poem's earlier mockery of Vulcan's wife as a whore, which is also a way of mocking Vulcan himself. The passage reaches its climax when we are shown how mistaken is the suggestion that

> *No foole would his owne harvest spoile, or burne!*

One fool would – Vulcan; and his foolishness is most striking when blandly expressed under the pretence of fairness in exonerating him from some of the crimes attributed to him:

> *I will not argue thee, from those, of guilt,*
> *For they were burnt, but to be better built.*

The comments of the Puritan Brethren are worked into the passage easily and naturally as a means of laughing at Vulcan; but their inclusion allows them to be laughed at too. They are not attacked directly, but made ludicrous by their own speeches. Their lack of moral discrimination is evident as they show equal hostility to prostitution, bear-baiting, dancing, and the drama. Intent on seeing the hand of God in everything, and confident that they understand His motives, they are nevertheless unable to agree with each other. Moreover, the god who is moving in so mysterious a way is, to mock them still further, a pagan god. Perhaps the Puritans were easy game (I am tempted to adopt their own providential outlook and think of them as God's gift to the seventeenth-century satirist); but this is one of the finest pieces of satire they inspired.

I have already mentioned that the '*Execration*' demands considerable knowledge (or access to Herford and Simpson's eleventh volume) from the modern reader. But it is possible to exaggerate the amount of knowledge required (we can gather all we need to know of Bess Broughton,[1] for instance, from the poem itself), and the very requirement points to a strength we often find in Jonson. The poem,

---

1. Line 216.

typically, is an amalgam of classical learning, detailed contemporary reference, and personal reactions; and these are the means by which what started as a private disaster becomes a public joke with ramifications far beyond the personal and far beyond a joke.

Jonson's verse-epistles particularly show how personal and public concerns may be combined. '*An Epistle answering to one that asked to be Sealed of the Tribe of Ben*'[1] helps us to understand the relation in which Jonson stood to his 'Sons' and the great influence he had on them. Moreover, the moral implications of this poem, with its praise of self-sufficiency and stoicism,[2] are obviously of more than personal interest. The poet shows himself aware of contemporary political problems, when he mentions them to stress that they cannot affect the ideal man he describes:

> *What is't to me whether the French Designe*
> *Be, or be not, to get the* Val-telline?
> (31-2)

The poem consists principally of advice and, it must be admitted, self-glorification. Nevertheless, if this advice and self-glorification are not offensive, it is mainly because here, as always in Jonson's epistles, the tone is personal as well as public. Jonson never forgets he is addressing primarily one other person, and we are always aware as we read the poem of the recipient and of his relation to the writer. We can expect advice when a middle-aged and famous poet is writing to a young admirer, and the advice is the more acceptable since it is given with touches of humour and even an occasional hint of modesty. Also, behind the offering of the advice lie the hope and faith that it will be taken, and this is a compliment to the recipient.

The Biblical allusion in the title[3] has a touch of self-deprecating humour. The alternative interpretation, that it shows a blasphemous megalomania, strikes me as very unlikely since uncharacteristic. The poem that follows is mainly an expansion of the thought of the first lines:

> *Men that are safe, and sure, in all they doe,*

---

1. Herford, VIII, 218.
2. Herford, II, 374: '... the virus of the Inigo affair now only gives an acid relish to the temper of lofty and disdainful self-sufficiency which was the noblest answer within his compass to the tyranny of man and fate.'
3. *Revelation*, VII. 8.

> *Care not what trials they are put unto;*
> *They meet the fire, the Test, as Martyrs would;*
> *And though Opinion stampe them not, are gold.*
> (1–4)

There is evidence here, of course, that the religious allusion in the title is not merely a joke: it prepares us for the moralizing which follows. Jonson continues, typically, to expand on the ideal presented in the first lines by giving a catalogue of people who fall short of it and thus show it up by contrast. This catalogue shows Jonson's ability to coin terse phrases like 'the wild Anarchie of Drinke'[1] and make sudden satiric thrusts like the one at those who seek a 'Sealing'[2] very different from that mentioned in the title:

> *That never yet did friend, or friendship seeke*
> *But for a Sealing...*
> (14–15)

or like the one at ignoramuses who profess knowledge:

> *That censure all the Towne, and all th' affaires,*
> *And know whose ignorance is more then theirs;*
> (23–4)

and, naturally, at Inigo Jones in an attack which, lacking subtlety, does not lack force:

> *...my Fame, to his, not under-heares,*
> *That guides the Motions, and directs the beares.*
> (49–50)

By the time Jonson comes to Inigo Jones he has already moved back from his survey of satirized types to Jonson. His outline of his own character and ideals, although it reveals a high opinion of himself, is not at all offensive. I think this is not so much because of the phrase 'mine owne fraile Pitcher' of which Herford and Simpson say:

The danger of supersession at Court has made Jonson unusually modest.[3]

---

1. Line 10.
2. That is, ask someone to become surety for a loan.
3. Herford, XI, 86.

This is merely mock-modesty. No, we accept this self-glorification really because it is a disarmingly honest piece of self-revelation, and a compliment to the recipient: Jonson cannot have been unaware that he was revealing not only his stoic ideal but also the difficulty he had in living up to it, when he wrote:

> *But that's a blow, by which in time I may*
> *Lose all my credit with my Christmas Clay,*
> *And animated* Porc'lane *of the Court,*
> *I, and for this neglect, the courser sort*
> *Of earthen Jarres, there may molest me too:*
> *Well, with mine owne fraile Pitcher, what to doe*
> *I have decreed; keepe it from waves, and presse;*
> *Lest it be justled, crack'd, made nought, or lesse:*
> *Live to that point I will, for which I am man,*
> *And dwell as in my Center, as I can,*
> *Still looking to, and ever loving heaven;*
> *With reverence using all the gifts then⟨ce⟩ given.*
> (51–62)

The poem continues with a magnificently sensuous image (drawn appropriately from the Court entertainments which have been mentioned previously) in which true friends are contrasted with false ones:

> *'Mongst which, if I have any friendships sent,*
> *Such as are square, wel-tagde, and permanent,*
> *Not built with Canvasse, paper, and false lights,*
> *As are the Glorious Scenes, at the great sights;*
> *And that there be no fev'ry heats, nor colds,*
> *Oylie Expansions, or shrunke durtie folds,*
> *But all so cleare, and led by reasons flame,*
> *As but to stumble in her sight were shame;*
> *These I will honour, love, embrace, and serve:*
> *And free it from all question to preserve.*
> (63–72)

After this powerful summary of what has gone before, the poem ends with a return to the request which inspired the poem. Here the short sentences, the pauses dictated by the syntax, and the enjambement add dignity and importance to the granting of the request:

> *So short you read my Character, and theirs*
> *I would call mine, to which not many Staires*
> *Are asked to climbe. First give me faith, who know*
> *My selfe a little. I will take you so,*
> *As you have writ your selfe. Now stand, and then,*
> *Sir, you are Sealed of the Tribe of Ben.*
>
> (73–8)

It is probably because Jonson cannot help attacking someone, even when he is writing a eulogy, and even when it is a eulogy of himself, that 'the pervasive heroic and idealizing strain'[1] in his poetry often receives less than its due. A poem to the Countess of Rutland[2] includes – after a typical mixture of invective against 'almightie gold',[3] flatterers and timeservers,[4] and 'noble ignorants'[5] – a fine passage which is one of many reminding us that Jonson believed it was an important function of poetry to preserve the memory of greatness:

> *How many equall with the Argive Queene,*
> *Haue beautie knowne, yet none so famous seene?*
> *Achilles was not first, that valiant was,*
> *Or, in an armies head, that, lock't in brasse,*
> *Gaue killing strokes. There were braue men, before*
> *Aiax, or Idomen, or all the store,*
> *That Homer brought to Troy; yet none so liue:*
> *Because they lack'd the sacred pen, could giue*
> *Like life vnto 'hem. Who heau'd Hercvles*
> *Vnto the starres? or the Tyndarides?*
> *Who placed Iasons Argo in the skie?*
> *Or set bright Ariadnes crowne so high?*
> *Who made a lampe of Berenices hayre?*

---

1. Jonas A. Barish, review of Trimpi, *M.P.*, LXI, No. 3 (1962), 242.
2. Herford, VIII, 113.
3. Line 2.
4. Lines 1–18.
5. Line 28.

Or lifted Cassiopea in her chayre?
But onely Poets, rapt with rage diuine?[1]
(49–63)

I hope that a consideration of three poems, glorifying a place, a titled lady, and a poet, will show the skill and variety of his commendatory verse.

Jonson's poem 'To Penshvrst'[2] is, like all his work, well grounded in antiquity,[3] and, like very much of it, a poem that has had many successors in English.[4] Although it is therefore interesting both as an instance of how Jonson used his sources and for its influence on subsequent English poetry, I wish to discuss it in its own right as one of Jonson's finest poems.

'To Penshvrst' may be described briefly as a poem in praise of a country house and estate and the people who live there; but it is important that this praise goes far beyond the immediate and personal to suggest a whole way of life, even a whole civilization. For Jonson, as for many of his contemporaries, Sir Philip Sidney was the embodiment of a civilized way of life.[5] Here, since Sir Philip's brother, Robert, was the owner of the estate when Jonson wrote the poem, the whole family comes to stand for this civilized way of life. A tree on the estate is a reminder of the greatest member of that family and of his greatest achievement, as a poet:

That taller tree, which of a nut was set,
At his great birth, where all the Muses met.
(13–14)

Other features of the estate emphasize where true worth lies, in moral living rather than in mere ostentation:

---

1. These lines are a reworking of Horace, *Odes* IV.9 ('Ne forte credas . . .'), especially lines 13–28 (Loeb edition, 1964, pp. 318–20). The notion is, of course, a commonplace; it is the importance of it to Jonson I am stressing.

2. Herford, VIII, 93.

3. H. A. Mason, *op. cit.*, pp. 273–9, discusses Jonson's borrowings from Martial in this poem. Paul M. Cubeta, 'A Jonsonian Ideal: "To Penshurst"', *P.Q.*, XLII No. 1 (January 1963), 14–24, discusses the borrowings from Martial and Juvenal.

4. Maurice Hussey, *op. cit.*, p. 6: 'The poem appears now as a *locus classicus* of the Cavalier school of poetic compliment and, far more than that, one of the seminal writings of the period.' Two poems which show the influence of 'To Penshvrst' very clearly are '*To Saxham*', *The Poems of Thomas Carew with his Masque Coelum Britannicum*, ed. Rhodes Dunlap, 1949, p. 27, and '*To my friend G.N. from* Wrest', *ibid.*, p. 86. The similarities and differences between these poems and 'To Penshvrst' and 'To Sir Robert Wroth' (Herford, VIII, 96) are discussed by Rufus A. Blanchard, 'Carew and Jonson', *S.P.*, LII (1955), 201–2.

5. Walton, p. 32.

> *...though thy walls be of the countrey stone,*
> *They' are rear'd with no mans ruine, no mans grone,*
> *There's none, that dwell about them, wish them downe ...*
> (45-7)

Throughout, the poem shows a delight in the estate both for its physical attractiveness and for its usefulness, economic and moral, especially to those, 'the farmer, and the clowne',[1] whose welfare depends on it. What starts as sensuous description can become praise of fecundity and generosity:

> *Then hath thy orchard fruit, thy garden flowers,*
> *Fresh as the ayre, and new as are the houres.*
> *The earely cherry, with the later plum,*
> *Fig, grape, and quince, each in his time doth come:*
> *The blushing apricot, and woolly peach*
> *Hang on thy walls that euery child may reach.*
> (39-44)

Jonson's inclusion of classical divinities among the inhabitants of Penshurst has been objected to as artificial and inappropriate.[2] I think it is artistic and appropriate: the poem moves throughout on the two planes of physical description and moral inference from this description; details of the contemporary English scene are present both literally and as symbols, and the classical divinities are symbolically, or heraldically, present:

> *Thou hast thy walkes for health, as well as sport:*
> *Thy* Mount, *to which the* Dryads *doe resort,*
> *Where Pan, and Bacchvs their high feasts haue made,*
> *Beneath the broad beech, and the chest-nut shade;*
> *That taller tree, which of a nut was set,*
> *At his great birth, where all the* Muses *met.*
> *There, in the writhed barke, are cut the names*
> *Of many a Sylvane, taken with his flames.*
> *And thence, the ruddy* Satyres *oft prouoke*
> *The lighter* Faunes, *to reach thy* Ladies Oke.

---

1. Line 48.
2. Herford, II, 369; H. A. Mason, *op. cit.*, p. 276.

> *Thy copp's too, nam'd of Gamage, thou hast there,*
> *That neuer failes to serue thee season'd deere ...*
> (9–20)

Since we can accept the '*Dryads*' easily (they may well be a flattering reference to the ladies of the house), and since we are already familiar with the '*Muses*' from many other English poems, it is not difficult to accept the other divinities as figuratively present.

Another objection sometimes made to the poem is that the animals on the estate are there to be eaten.[1] To complain of Jonson's emphasis on this is to show a complete misunderstanding of the poem. 'The purpled pheasant' and 'painted partrich', however attractive in appearance, are valued most because they have their appropriate place in the scheme of things, to help others to stay alive; to praise them for their good looks alone would be to praise mere ostentation. Worse than that, the poem would lose contact with reality and degenerate from a praise of civilization to mere whimsy. The beasts are a necessity, without which the good life is not possible.[2]

Herford and Simpson object, however, not so much that the animals are eaten, as that they are 'eager for the honour of furnishing the the table of the Sidneys'.[3] Taken literally this would, of course, be ridiculous. But it is clear from the tone of this passage that Jonson is here making playful use of the superstition that all creatures recognized their superiors in the 'Chain of Being'[4] and obeyed them willingly:

> *... the topps*
> *Fertile of wood, Ashore, and Sydney's copp's,*
> *To crowne thy open table, doth prouide*
> *The purpled pheasant, with the speckled side:*
> *The painted partrich lyes in euery field,*
> *And, for thy messe, is willing to be kill'd.*
> *And if the high-swolne* Medway *faile thy dish,*
> *Thou hast thy ponds, that pay thee tribute fish,*
> *Fat, aged carps, that runne into thy net.*
> *And pikes, now weary their owne kinde to eat,*

---

1. Smith, p. 234.
2. H. A. Mason, *op. cit.*, p. 278.
3. Herford, II, 369.
4. E. M. W. Tillyard, *The Elizabethan World Picture*, 1943, fourth impression 1948, p. 32.

> *As loth, the second draught, or cast to stay,*
> *Officiously, at first, themselues betray.*
> *Bright eeles, that emulate them, and leape on land,*
> *Before the fisher, or into his hand.*
>
> (25–38)

Clearly, the eels are the most enthusiastic of all. Before we come to them, Jonson has gradually accustomed us to the notion which he wants us to accept as an amusing extravaganza suggestive of great fertility and skill in hunting. At first it is the wood that 'doth prouide' the pheasants, and the verb shows only a touch of personification. Then the partridge is said to be 'willing to be kill'd' as a way of complimenting the Sidneys, since it is 'for *thy* messe'.[1] To say that the carps 'runne into thy net', although it hints at volition, is also an accurate description of how they are caught. We have now been prepared for the dutifulness of the pikes; and anyway the comment on them also may be taken as a compliment to the fisherman. After all this it would show an unexpected individuality on the part of the eels if they did not 'leape on land'.[2]

This poem has many features which are typical of Jonson. There is the tendency to praise by means of derision of the opposite, as in the first lines of the poem and in the incidental stroke of satire which occurs in the praise of Lady Sidney's chastity:

> *Thy lady's noble, fruitfull, chaste withall.*
> *His children thy great lord may call his owne:*
> *A fortune, in this age, but rarely knowne.*
>
> (90–2)

There is also the exactness and discrimination in praising, as in the passage mentioning the entertainment of the King and his son:

> *What (great, I will not say, but) sodayne cheare*
> *Did'st thou, then, make 'hem!*
>
> (82–3)

As a fitting conclusion, there is the typical contrast between two

---

1. My italics.

2. It is worth mentioning that eels do leave the ponds where they are born, after changing in colour from yellow to silver ('Bright eeles'), and travel considerable distances overland. See T. T. Macan and E. B. Worthington, *Life in Lakes and Rivers*, 1951, reprinted 1962, pp. 186–7.

words, 'built' and 'dwells', after the meaning of both of those words has been defined in the course of the poem:

> *Now, Penshvrst, they that will proportion thee*
> *With other edifices, when they see*
> *Those proud, ambitious heaps, and nothing else,*
> *May say, their lords haue built, but thy lord dwells.*
> (99–102)

A poem on a much smaller scale, which also shows Jonson's skill in elegant yet weighty compliment, is 'To Lvcy, Covntesse of Bedford, with Mr. Donnes Satyres'.[1] The poem opens with an exclamatory compliment to the Countess of Bedford which plays on the derivation (*lux*) of her Christian name:

> *Lvcy, you brightnesse of our spheare, who are*
> *Life of the* Muses *day, their morning-starre!*

The poem concludes with a variation of these two lines:

> *Lvcy, you brightnesse of our spheare, who are*
> *The* Muses *euening, as their morning-starre.*

Both the change in the metaphor used for the Countess of Bedford from morning star to evening star (an acceptable change since they are, of course, the same star), and the fact that these couplets stand at the beginning and end of a discussion of poetry, emphasize that she is 'Life of the *Muses* day'.[2]

The lines between the opening and closing couplets show how the compliment is justified and, since they contain argument, the rhythm is more complex, slowed down by the turns of the thought. The famous gnomic sentence which ends the following passage owes its effect not only to the double meaning of 'rare' (valuable and scarce) but also to its being allowed to run out freely, with its last word emphasized by the rhyme, after the previous lines have been slowed down by periodic construction, parenthesis, and enjambement:

> *If workes (not th' authors) their owne grace should looke,*
> *Whose poems would not wish to be your booke?*

---

1. Herford, VIII, 60.
2. There is an interesting account of the Countess of Bedford as a patron of letters in John Buxton, *Sir Philip Sidney and the English Renaissance*, 1954, pp. 224–33.

> *But these, desir'd by you, the makers ends*
> *Crowne with their owne. Rare poemes aske rare friends.*

Similar methods are used to slow down the movement of the later lines which come to a climax in the clause, flat out of context but very powerful in the poem, 'best are you':

> *They, then, that liuing where the matter is bred,*
> *Dare for these poems, yet, both aske, and read,*
> *And like them too; must needfully, though few,*
> *Be of the best: and 'mongst those, best are you.*

The poem is a good example of Jonson's ability to compliment highly without compromising his own high standards and his own dignity. It is typical too, in that, although highly-coloured or unusual imagery is avoided, there is still the element of surprise, as in the shock which 'And like them too' gives when read in its context at the beginning of a line and as a parenthesis in a periodic sentence. The poem is primarily a compliment to the Countess of Bedford; but, while it compliments her in terms that are personally most appropriate and in a manner that makes the compliment seem almost a necessity, it also manages without any sense of strain to pay respect to the dignity of poetry and to one poet in particular. A discussion of it makes a fitting prelude to what is probably Jonson's greatest triumph in complimentary verse.

The long commendatory poem which Jonson wrote for the First Folio of Shakespeare's works, 'To the memory of my beloued, The AVTHOR Mr. William Shakespeare: And what he hath left vs',[1] has been frequently praised,[2] especially for its abundance of terse, memorable phrases: 'Soule of the Age',[3] '*Marlowes* mighty line',[4] 'small *Latine*, and lesse *Greeke*',[5] 'gentle *Shakespeare*',[6] 'Sweet Swan of *Auon!*',[7] to mention only those most often quoted. But critics seem to fight shy of any detailed analysis of the poem as a whole.

---

1. Herford, VIII, 390. In the course of my discussion I quote all of this poem.
2. E.g. Herford, II, 377–8; Smith, pp. 235–6; G.B. Johnston, *Poems of Ben Jonson*, p. xl; Kenneth Muir 'Changing Interpretations of Shakespeare', *A Guide to English Literature*, Vol. II *The Age of Shakespeare*, ed. Boris Ford, pp. 285, 299.
3. Line 17.
4. Line 30.
5. Line 31.
6. Line 56.
7. Line 71.

Herford and Simpson's description of it as 'rather a song of triumph than an elegy'[1] is suggestive, but they make little attempt to expand on this remark. Again, Hugh Kenner's remark about lines 55–65 is suggestive but not pursued:

> The racy ease of expression is as typically Jonson's as the studied refusal to invent a new thing to say.[2]

Given that the expression is 'racy' (indeed much of it out of context is commonplace), and that the ideas and imagery in the poem are not new, what gives the poem its distinction?

It is hardly helpful, in fact it would be damning to the poem if it were true, to suggest that the poem owes its success to the greatness of its subject.[3] The most fervent admirer of Donne would hardly argue that the bulk of the elegies on him were other than mediocre, and indeed, what does Shakespeare's greatness do for William Basse's elegy?[4] The most that I think we can say on these lines is that we have here a subject to whom the most extravagant terms of praise seem appropriate, and that in this poem Jonson has perhaps the most suitable subject for praise he ever had – a man he admired for his frankness and honesty, a poet more than worthy of the greatest praise, and one more opportunity to comment on the dignity of poetry. It is worth studying in detail how he seized this chance.

At the start, the poet winds into his subject deliberately slowly; the rhythm is hesitant and the tone thoughtful. It is not that Jonson is uncertain what to praise Shakespeare for;[5] he is making it plain that his praise, when it comes, will be intelligent and discriminating, that it will be worth having:

> *To draw no enuy* (Shakespeare) *on thy name,*
> *Am I thus ample to thy Booke, and Fame:*
> *While I confesse thy writings to be such,*
> *As neither* Man, *nor* Muse, *can praise too much.*
> *'Tis true, and all mens suffrage. But these wayes*
> *Were not the paths I meant vnto thy praise:*

---

1. Herford, II, 378.
2. *Op. cit.*, p. xxiii.
3. Trimpi, p. 148: '. . . certain lines such as "He was not of an age, but for all time!" encourage readers to praise the poem for an intensity of feeling derived from their own response to Shakespeare . . .'
4. Quoted from in Herford, XI, 145.
5. As suggested in Trimpi, pp. 148–51.

> *For seeliest Ignorance on these may light,*
> *Which, when it sounds at best, but eccho's right;*
> *Or blinde Affection, which doth ne're aduance*
> *The truth, but gropes, and vrgeth all by chance;*
> *Or crafty Malice, might pretend this praise,*
> *And thinke to ruine, where it seem'd to raise.*
> *These are, as some infamous Baud, or Whore,*
> *Should praise a Matron. What could hurt her more?*
> *But thou art proofe against them, and indeed*
> *Aboue th'ill fortune of them, or the need.*
>
> (1–16)

As usual, Jonson cannot praise one person without dispraising others; but the nice discrimination between 'seeliest Ignorance', 'blinde Affection', and 'crafty Malice', and between their different ways of failing, is a method of making us more discriminating and judicious in our attitude to the intelligent praise about to follow. The lines are thoughtful and authoritative in tone, as here with the balance of 'thinke' and 'seem'd' and (helped by the alliteration) of 'ruine' and 'raise':

> *And thinke to ruine, where it seem'd to raise.*

Above all, we hear the tone of the speaking voice and sense a real man behind the words; this is most obvious with the rhetorical question 'What could hurt her more?' and the sudden addition to a sentence which seemed completed, 'or the need'.

The passage that follows is the first piece of sustained praise in the poem:

> *I, therefore will begin. Soule of the Age!*
> *The applause! delight! the wonder of our Stage!*
> *My Shakespeare, rise; I will not lodge thee by*
> *Chaucer, or Spenser, or bid Beaumont lye*
> *A little further, to make thee a roome:*
> *Thou art a Moniment, without a tombe,*
> *And art aliue still, while thy Booke doth liue,*
> *And we haue wits to read, and praise to giue.*
>
> (17–24)

However, this is not simply praise. The surprising remark 'I, therefore will begin', with its suggestion of irony, the exclamations which follow in rapid succession, and most of all what Herford and Simpson praise, 'the scornful development of Basse's quaint conceit',[1] complicate the tone. The passage Jonson is mocking occurs in another poem in praise of Shakespeare:

> *Renowned Spenser, lye a thought more nye*
> *To learned Chaucer, and rare Beaumont lye*
> *A little nearer Spenser to make roome*
> *ffor Shakespeare in your threefold fowerfold Tombe.*[2]

Jonson is simultaneously praising Shakespeare and deriding those who cannot praise him worthily. The exclamations mock 'seeliest Ignorance', 'blinde Affection', and 'crafty Malice', and of course the subsequent passage mocks William Basse, although it is worth mentioning that the passage has this mocking tone even if we do not know Basse's poem; we need only read it with emphasis on 'I' – '*I* will not lodge thee ...'

The method here is very similar to that employed by Jonson in his poem to Drayton.[3] This also is a complimentary poem, but J. W. Hebel has argued that it is 'sly satire rather than compliment',[4] and Herford and Simpson say:

> The truth is that Jonson by his extravagance has done Drayton an injustice, and lovers of Drayton, resenting this, have sought to readjust the focus of the poem. Why did Drayton print the lines? Apparently he took them seriously and, on Mr Hebel's view, was something of a simpleton.[5]

The key-lines for both interpretations are these:

> *Lend me thy voyce, O Fame, that I may draw*
> *Wonder to truth! and haue my Vision hoorld*
> *Hot from thy trumpet, round, about the world.*
> (12–14)

There is a touch of satire here, but not of Drayton. The position of this passage in the poem is similar to the position of the passage I am

---

1. Herford, II, 378.
2. Herford, XI, 145.
3. 'THE VISION OF Ben. Jonson, ON THE MUSES OF HIS FRIEND M. Drayton', Herford, VIII, 396.
4. 'Drayton's *Sirena*', *P.M.L.A.*, XXXIX (1924), 830–2; my quotation is from p. 830.
5. Herford, XI, 149.

discussing from the Shakespeare poem. In the passage from the poem to Drayton Jonson is simultaneously praising Drayton and mocking those attacked in the opening lines:

> It hath beene question'd, Michael, if I bee
> A Friend at all; or, if at all, to thee:
> Because, who make the question, haue not seene
> Those ambling visits, passe in verse, betweene
> Thy Muse, and mine, as they expect. 'Tis true:
> You haue not writ to me, nor I to you;
> And, though I now begin, 'tis not to rub
> Hanch against Hanch, or raise a riming Club
> About the towne: this reck'ning I will pay,
> Without conferring symboles. This's my day.
>
> (1–10)

'This's my day' helps to establish a similar tone to that established by 'I, therefore will begin'. Also, much of the Drayton poem consists of exclamations, rare in Jonson but similar to those in the passage from the poem to Shakespeare. In both poems Jonson's characteristic method of praising one person by deriding another is brought to a height.

The poem to Shakespeare continues with what is probably its most famous passage:

> That I not mixe thee so, my braine excuses;
> I meane with great, but disproportion'd Muses:
> For, if I thought my iudgement were of yeeres,
> I should commit thee surely with thy peeres,
> And tell, how farre thou didst our Lily out-shine,
> Or sporting Kid, or Marlowes mighty line.
> And though thou hadst small Latine, and lesse Greeke,
> From thence to honour thee, I would not seeke
> For names; but call forth thund'ring Æschilus,
> Euripides, and Sophocles to vs,
> Paccuuius, Accius, him of Cordoua dead,
> To life againe, to heare thy Buskin tread,
> And shake a Stage: Or, when thy Sockes were on,
> Leaue thee alone, for the comparison

> *Of all, that insolent* Greece, *or haughtie* Rome
> *Sent forth, or since did from their ashes come.*
> (25–40)

This is, of course, of great historical interest, because it places
Shakespeare so firmly in the high position we now know he deserves.
It is also of poetical interest, for the manner in which this placing is
done. The first two lines show a characteristic discrimination and
judgement. Perhaps they apply more to Jonson's ideal of the poet
than to his sober judgement of Shakespeare; but the poem is here
moving out from a consideration of one poet to deal with the great
ideal Jonson always kept in mind. Here, as in several later passages
from the poem, it is as well to bear in mind the indulgence Jonson
asked for his *Epigrammes*:

> . . . *if all answere not, in all numbers, the pictures I haue made of*
> *them: I hope it will be forgiuen me, that they are no ill pieces, though*
> *they be not like the persons.*[1]

Trimpi objects that 'if I thought my iudgement were of yeeres' is
'uncharacteristic and unnecessary',[2] but W. B. Hunter's interpretation
is more satisfactory – 'i.e. over the course of many years: beyond the
Elizabethans named back to the classical writers'.[3] The puns on names
– 'sporting *Kid*' and 'shake a Stage' – are most appropriate to the
exultant mood of the passage.[4] So too is another pun, one which seems
to have passed generally unnoticed. Surely when he wrote 'thou didst
our *Lily* out-shine' Jonson was thinking of the brightness of the
flower he was later to describe as 'the Plant, and flowre of light'.[5]

The next passage in the poem is an expansion of the preceding one,
both in its insistence on Shakespeare's pre-eminence and in its other
purpose as a transition to further consideration of Jonson's ideal
writer:

> *Triúmph, my* Britaine, *thou hast one to showe,*
> *To whom all Scenes of* Europe *homage owe.*

1. Herford, VIII, 26.
2. Trimpi, p. 150.
3. *The Complete Poetry of Ben Jonson*, ed. W. B. Hunter, 1963, p. 373, footnote 7.
4. Contrast Herford, XI, 145: 'In such a context one cannot but regret the inane joke on the name of Kyd.'
5. '*To the immortall memorie, and friendship of that noble paire, Sir* Lvcivs Cary, *and Sir* H. Morison', Herford, VIII, 245.

> *He was not of an age, but for all time!*
>   *And all the* Muses *still were in their prime,*
> *When like* Apollo *he came forth to warme*
>   *Our eares, or like a* Mercury *to charme!*
> *Nature her selfe was proud of his designes,*
>   *And ioy'd to weare the dressing of his lines!*
> *Which were so richly spun, and wouen so fit,*
>   *As, since, she will vouchsafe no other* Wit.
> *The merry* Greeke, *tart* Aristophanes,
>   *Neat* Terence, *witty* Plautus, *now not please;*
> *But antiquated, and deserted lye*
>   *As they were not of Natures family.*
>   (41–54)

Most remarkable here is how Jonson makes such a striking line out of 'ten low words':[1]

> *He was not of an age, but for all time!*

This line owes much of its effect to its context where 'of an age' reminds of the previous mention of Lyly, Kyd, and Marlowe from whom Shakespeare learned so much, and 'for all time' summarizes all that is suggested of his pre-eminence in the comparisons with the great classical writers. In or out of context (and we must remember that this line is often quoted by itself) much of the effectiveness comes from the contrast between the mere prepositions 'of' and 'for', the first implying dependence and the second influence.

Jonson continues with an account of the creative struggle which, while it is probably more applicable to his own methods than to Shakespeare's, is included as appropriate to his ideal poet:

> *Yet must I not giue Nature all: Thy Art,*
>   *My gentle* Shakespeare, *must enioy a part.*
> *For though the* Poets *matter, Nature be,*
>   *His Art doth giue the fashion. And, that he,*
> *Who casts to write a liuing line, must sweat,*
>   *(Such as thine are) and strike the second heat*
> *Vpon the* Muses *anuile: turne the same,*
>   *(And himselfe with it) that he thinkes to frame;*

---

1. Pope, 'An Essay on Criticism', line 347, *op. cit.*, p. 154.

Or for the Lawrell, he may gaine a scorne,
For a good Poet's made, as well as borne.
And such wert thou. Looke how the fathers face
Liues in his issue, euen so, the race
Of Shakespeares minde, and manners brightly shines
In his well torned, and true-filed lines:
In each of which, he seemes to shake a Lance,
As brandish't at the eyes of Ignorance.

(55–70)

Here a sense of the difficulty and struggle involved is given by the rhythm which is slowed down by the syntax, the enjambement, and the parentheses, especially that parenthesis which occurs in an unexpected place – '(Such as thine are)'. One parenthesis, '(And himselfe with it)', is a shrewd statement of the psychological difficulty there is in rewriting, reminiscent of Yeats's lines:

> The friends that have it I do wrong
> When ever I remake a song,
> Should know what issue is at stake:
> It is myself that I remake.[1]

In the conclusion to the poem Jonson first speaks of Shakespeare as a swan, which is fitting considering his birthplace, and then, taking up a hint contained in two previous phrases, 'our *Lily* outshine'[2] and 'brightly shines',[3] makes the swan become the constellation Cygnus. Like so much else in the poem, the images are far from original; but they are not meant to be original, only peculiarly appropriate in their context. The word 'influence' (which means here both literary and stellar influence) adds force to the phrase 'Starre of *Poets*', for instance, and the last word of the poem, 'light', summarizes all the praise of Shakespeare and is in sharp contrast to the previous use of the same word in a different sense:

For seeliest Ignorance on these may light,[4]

and to the previous mention of 'blinde Affection'.[5]

---

1. *The Variorum Edition of the Poems of W.B. Yeats*, ed. Peter Allt and Russell K. Alspach, second printing 1965, p. 778.
2. Line 29.
3. Line 67.
4. Line 7.
5. Line 9.

Sweet Swan of Auon! *what a sight it were*
    To see thee in our waters yet appeare,
And make those flights vpon the bankes of Thames,
    That so did take Eliza, *and our* Iames!
But stay, I see thee in the Hemisphere
    Aduanc'd, and made a Constellation there!
Shine forth, thou Starre of Poets, *and with rage,*
    Or influence, chide, or cheere the drooping Stage;
Which, since thy flight from hence, hath mourn'd like night,
    And despaires day, but for thy Volumes light.
               (71–80)

Jonson was obviously not one of those who assume that occasional
poetry is only occasionally poetry. It is one of the strengths of his best
work that, while it is aware of ideals and aspirations, it always relates
them to the human and ordinary. He shows us men and women both
as they are and as they ought to be. Sometimes, and especially in his
poem on Shakespeare, he shows us reality approximating to the ideal.

4
'Lyrick Sweetnesse in an Ode, or Sonnet'[1]

Some few of Jonson's lyrics are probably more widely known than any of his other poems. Yet even his lyrics do not always meet with unqualified approval. Swinburne says:

> . . . the flowers of his growing have every quality but one which belongs to the rarest and finest among flowers: they have colour, form, variety, fertility, vigour: the one thing they want is fragrance . . . That singing power which answers in verse to the odour of a blossom, to the colouring of a picture, to the flavour of a fruit, – that quality without which they may be good, commendable, admirable, but cannot be delightful, – was not, it should seem, a natural gift of this great writer's . . .[2]

Behind the 'singing power' which Swinburne tries to demonstrate in his own prose, there is criticism unconsciously shrewd. Jonson's lyrics are not meant to seem artless or 'natural' and, to some tastes, there may well be something repellent in the very success of a poem which is

> *So polisht, perfect, round, and even*
> *As it slid moulded off from Heaven.*[3]

Certainly this is something which it takes more effort to appreciate than does 'the odour of a blossom'. Herford and Simpson may be right when they say that Jonson was 'the least lyric personality of his time',[4] especially if a 'lyric personality' has to be someone like Goethe, Heine, or Burns, someone with a remarkable ability for falling in love and out of it, and for recording these actions with diary-like regularity and apparent naivety. Despite the fact that many of Jonson's lyrics are ostensibly love-poems, it would be misleading to describe him as a love-poet; there is passion in his lyrics, but it is the passion for artistic perfection.

---

1. William Hodgson, 'ON THE AUTHOR, *The Poet Laureat*, Ben Jonson', Herford, XI, 351.
2. Swinburne, p. 4.
3. 'EUPHEME', Herford, VIII, 280.
4. Herford, I, 115.

I have already suggested, with reference to Jonson's poems to Charis, that it is immaterial whether or not Jonson did fall in love at the age of fifty.[1] We shall be less tempted to bother with this biographical question if we remember that Horace had also suffered (or, to credit him with imagination too, had written of suffering) from the same affliction at the same age. It was probably Horace whom Jonson was particularly alluding to when he wrote:

I have had, and have my Peeres.[2]

Jonson's poems to Charis are following an honoured literary precedent, and that is what matters most.[3]

In fact, Jonson translated the relevant ode from Horace.[4] His translation[5] is striking and satisfactory in itself, but even more striking when it is compared to the original. It is often said that translations of verse into verse may, like wives, be either faithful or beautiful but not both. We naturally expect that a poet who is above all intent on writing a good poem in his own language will mould his material into something very different from the original; I have already discussed some instances of Jonson's doing just this.[6] His translation of 'Intermissa, Venus . . .', however, is a different kind of achievement. His version is so accurate that it might well be used as a crib for the original. The Latin idiom is preserved when this is possible without its seeming un-English, as in 'not without the Flute' for 'non sine fistula', or changed into English idiom without losing any of its meaning or force, as when 'et pro sollicitis non tacitus reis' becomes 'And for the troubled Clyent fyl's his tongue'. Again and again the extraordinary felicity of Horace's phrasing is matched in the English: 'dulcium/mater saeva Cupidinum' becomes 'Sower Mother of sweet Loves'; 'spes animi credula mutui' becomes 'credulous hope of mutuall Joy'; 'thin teares' is just right for 'rara . . . lacrima'.

It is true that here Jonson, unusually for him, does not always keep to the normal English prose word-order. Yet there is no variation

---

1. See p. 30 above.
2. '*His Excuse for loving*', Herford, VIII, 131.
3. It is not a slavish adherence to precedent, of course. Apart from everything else, Charis is a woman, Horace's Ligurinus a boy.
4. *Odes*, IV.I, ('Intermissa, Venus, diu . . .'), Loeb edition, p. 282.
5. Herford, VIII, 292.
6. See above, pp. 22–7.

of this beyond what was common in poetry and, more important, he is not forced to wrest his words from their usual order by the demands of his verse-form or his insistence on verbal accuracy: he is working deliberately for a rhetorical purpose which includes an approximation to the effect of the original where the placing of the phrases is so important. In these two lines, for instance, 'among' is out of its usual place, 'With an uncomely silence' would not often in speech have its present position, and 'failes' would normally come after 'my tongue':

> *Or why, my well-grac'd words among,*
> *With an uncomely silence failes my tongue?*

But Jonson (with, it must be stressed, only such a variation of English prose word-order as is quite common in verse) is reproducing at least a little of the involuted effect of the Horace:

> *cur facunda parum decoro*
> *inter verba cadit lingua silentio?*

It is surprising how much Jonson does preserve of the shape of the original. The placing of the phrase 'With thy bright Swans' here:

> *More timely hie thee to the house,*
> *With thy bright Swans, of* Paulus Maximus:
> *There jest, and feast,*

is similar to the placing of the corresponding phrase in the original:

> *tempestivius in domum*
> *Pauli, purpureis ales oloribus,*
> *comissabere Maximi ...*

The very movement of Horace's verse – the stops and starts of the syntax, and the enjambement – is reflected in the Jonson. We may, for instance, compare his first five lines:

> Venus, *againe thou mov'st a warre*
> *Long intermitted, pray thee, pray thee spare:*
> *I am not such, as in the Reigne*
> *Of the good* Cynara *I was: Refraine,*
> *Sower Mother of sweet Loves,*

with Horace's:

> *Intermissa, Venus, diu*
> *rursus bella moves. parce, precor, precor.*

> *non sum qualis eram bonae*
> *sub regno Cinarae. desine, dulcium*
>
> *mater saeva Cupidinium . . .*

Again, the end of Jonson's poem enacts in its rhythm the yearning which is its subject; it seems to stretch out:

> *I dreame every Night*
> *I hold thee fast! but fled hence, with the Light,*
> *Whether in Mars his field thou bee,*
> *Or Tybers winding streames, I follow thee.*

So does the Latin:

> *nocturnis ego somniis*
> *iam captum teneo, iam volucrem sequor*
> *te per gramina Martii*
> *Campi, te per aquas, dure, volubilis.*

Last but not least, Jonson's verse-form – alternate octosyllabic and decasyllabic lines rhyming in pairs – makes a good approximation to Horace's Second Asclepiadean where every second line is metrically an extension and slight variation of every first. In this, as in the details of his translation, Jonson knows just how far to go from his original in adapting it to English.

The lyrical skill which cannot be denied to Jonson may be admitted in terms which suggest that it is faintly indecent. He had, we are told, 'an extraordinary talent for simulating song'[1] and 'extraordinarily cunning artistry',[2] but lacked those qualities for which we value Shakespeare's[3] or Herrick's lyrics.[4] With Jonson we are usually aware of

> the conscious contrivance, the intellectualized pattern and style, of a scholarly poet.[3]

If we can take pleasure in 'clear-cut symmetry and diction',[5] then we shall enjoy Jonson's lyrics; if we look for love in a love-lyric, or passionate and tortured religious feelings in a hymn, we shall often

---

1. Herford, II, 339.
2. *Ibid.*, 340.
3. Douglas Bush, *Classical Influences in Renaissance Literature*, p. 39.
4. Swinburne, p. 98.
5. Douglas Bush, *Mythology and the Renaissance Tradition in English Poetry*, p. 88.

be disappointed. True, some of his lyrics have a biographical interest'
but the most striking feeling they communicate is one of delight in
artistic skill, a passion for perfection and completeness, for seeming
to say the last word.[1]

This skill may be seen particularly easily in lyrics whose matter
is so trivial that it does nothing to distract us from their manner.
One such is 'The Houre-glasse' :

> *Doe but consider this small dust,*
> *Here running in the Glasse,*
> *By Atomes mov'd;*
> *Could you beleeve, that this,*
> *The body 〈ever〉 was*
> *Of one that lov'd?*
> *And in his M*rs *flame, playing like a flye,*
> *Turn'd to cinders by her eye?*
> *Yes; and in death, as life, unblest,*
> *To have't exprest,*
> *Even ashes of lovers find no rest.*[2]

As Herford and Simpson point out, this is derived from a Renaissance
Latin poem:

> *Perspicuus vitro pulvis qui dividit horas,*
> *Dum vagus angustum saepe recurrit iter,*
> *Olim erat Alcippus: qui Gallae ut vidit ocellos*
> *Arsit et est subito factus ab igne cinis.*
> *Irrequiete cinis, miseros testabere amantes,*
> *More tuo, nulla posse quiete frui.*[3]

(The dust which, seen through this glass, allots the hours as, in its
restlessness, it returns repeatedly on its narrow path, was once
Alcippus: who, as soon as he saw Galla's eyes, burned and was
suddenly changed from fire to ashes. Restless ashes, you will
testify, by this habit of yours, that unhappy lovers can enjoy no
peace.)

---

1. Cf. Douglas Bush, *English Literature in the Earlier Seventeenth Century 1600–1660*,
p. 106: '... artistic feeling, if not love, refined and ordered in a pattern of delicate strength,
gives to his best lyrics a cool, assured poise, an idealism at once artificial and rational,
hardly less compelling in its way than emotional intensity...'
2. Herford, VIII, 148.
3. Herford, XI, 53.

Herford and Simpson quote two other English versions of this poem, one of them by Coleridge;[1] there is also a French version by Charles Vion de Dalibray (1600?–1653?).[2]

Clearly, the subject has some appeal. Nevertheless, it is a difficult one because of its triviality. Coleridge emphasizes the dangers that are there, simply by falling into them:

The Hour-Glass

> *O think, fair maid! these sands that pass*
> *In slender threads adown this glass,*
> *Were once the body of some swain,*
> *Who lov'd too well and lov'd in vain,*
> *And let one soft sigh heave thy breast,*
> *That not in life alone unblest*
> *E'en lovers' ashes find no rest.*

'In slender threads' is merely picturesque, and 'let one soft sigh heave thy breast' is more solemn than the occasion warrants; but the main weakness here is that Coleridge omits the conceit of the lover burned to ashes by his mistress' eyes and, while avoiding the problem of how to cope with this extravagant notion, falls into the error of leaving his poem obscure; to make it worse, even if we know the original we can imagine no way by which the lover can have become 'sands'.

In contrast, Jonson treats his subject with only as much seriousness as it can bear (which is not very much). His verse-form seems to me more suitable than the elegiacs of the Latin, it moves so lightly. Then Jonson gets the emphasis where he wants it, as in the last line where the weight (if we can talk of weight in such a fragile piece) comes gently, and appropriately, on 'ashes'.

Jonson strengthens the central conceit by adding the phrase 'playing like a flye'. He also makes the conceit more acceptable by admitting that it is hard to take:

> *Could you beleeve, that this,*
> *The body ⟨ever⟩ was*
> *Of one that lov'd?*
> *And in his M^rs flame, playing like a flye,*
> *Turn'd to cinders by her eye?*

1. *Ibid.*, 54.
2. *The Penguin Book of French Verse*, Vol. II, ed. Geoffrey Brereton (1958), p. 210.

His emphatic 'Yes' to his own question is in the same slightly mocking tone, as are the last three lines as a whole. Trimpi comments:

> By using the triple rhyme Jonson calls attention to the humorously stiff and quite superfluous pedagogical emphasis upon the meaning of the poem 'To have't exprest'.[1]

And one might add that 'exprest' is a Latinate pun ('put into words' and 'pressed out') with just the right touch of ironic pedantry.

To ask for passion, or philosophical or psychological or moral profundity, from such a poem would be to ensure disappointment. What we can enjoy is the verbal skill, the careful adjustment of the means to the end, the delicacy of the tone. And an appreciation of what such a lyric has to offer can make us more aware of the same qualities when we come across them in lyrics which have something to offer in other ways too.

In denying that such lyrics have moral profundity I am not, of course, denying them any relation to morals. It would certainly be strange if Jonson, so persistent a moralist everywhere else, were quite innocent of moral intention in his lyrics. I do not think it is stretching a point to suggest that the artistic perfection of such lyrics as '*The Houre-glasse*' implies a comment on the imperfections of the world. One way of seeing such lyrics is to regard them as visions of the perfection lost since the Fall: I have already mentioned how often Jonson uses the myth of the Golden Age as a symbol for perfection.[2]

Sometimes perfection is the subject-matter of his lyrics, and then we do not need to infer this ideal from the perfection of the verse alone. The reader who has the persistence to work his way through the sheer boredom of which *The New Inne* for the most part consists is eventually rewarded:

> *Seruant, what haue you there?* Lov. *A meditation,*
> *Or rather a vision, Madam, and of Beauty,*
> *Our former subiect.* Lad. *Pray you let vs heare it.*
>   Lov. *It was a beauty that I saw*
>   *So pure, so perfect, as the frame*
>   *Of all the vniuerse was lame,*

---

1. Trimpi, p. 280.
2. See pp. 84-5 above.

To that one figure, could I draw,
Or giue least line of it a law!

A skeine of silke without a knot!
A faire march made without a halt!
A curious forme without a fault!
A printed booke without a blot!
All beauty, and without a spot![1]

It is Lady Frampul who speaks first. Lovel's reply makes it clear that the subject of his poem is not so much one beauty as Beauty itself, the very idea or ideal of perfection.

In the second stanza four images are used to express this ideal. It is not Jonson's way to be extravagant with his imagery, and he uses so many images in order to suggest how very difficult it is to conceive of perfection. In fact, the first stanza implies the task is impossible. Again, as is usual with Jonson and as is inevitable in an imperfect world, the idea of perfection has to be expressed partly by negatives, by listing the faults (*'knot'*, *'halt'*, *'fault'*, *'blot'*) that perfection does not have: even the last line, which sums up the subject in the abstract word *'beauty'*, ends with the word *'spot'*.

As always, the syntax and verse-form contribute much to the effectiveness of the poem. The first stanza is one sentence containing strong pauses to suggest the difficulty of what the poet has to express:

So pure, so perfect, as the frame . . .

In contrast, the second stanza consists of a series of ejaculations as the attempt at expression is made again and again. The rhyme-scheme, in which each stanza ends with a couplet which rhymes with the first line of the stanza, is used in the first stanza to emphasize the effort required, and in the second to give a sense of finality and success.

The famous song from *Cynthias Reuells*, 'Qveene, *and* Huntresse, *chaste, and faire'*,[2] has a similar subject. It is in honour of Queen Elizabeth: she is Cynthia, the moon, the giver of light in darkness. Early in the play Cupid promises that Cynthia will appear 'with the full and royall expence of one of her cleerest moons'.[3] Later he says

---

1. Herford, VI, 468–9.
2. Herford, IV, 161.
3. *Ibid.*, 47.

that the foolish would-be courtiers, whom the play satirizes, '(like so many meteors) will vanish, when shee appeares'.[1] Cynthia's light is mentioned frequently in the play,[2] often with the implication that it is a spiritual rather than a physical light which, by filling the court with virtue and good sense, will dispel affectation and pride.

When Cynthia at last appears, 'The Hymne' is sung:

> Qveene, *and* Huntresse, *chaste, and faire,*
> *Now the* Sunne *is laid to sleepe,*
> *Seated, in thy siluer chaire,*
> *State in wonted manner keepe:*
> Hespervs *intreats thy light,*
> *Goddesse, excellently bright.*
>
> *Earth, let not thy enuious shade*
> *Dare it selfe to interpose;*
> Cynthias *shining orbe was made*
> *Heauen to cleere, when day did close:*
> *Blesse vs then with wished sight,*
> *Goddesse, excellently bright.*
>
> *Lay thy bow of pearle apart,*
> *And thy cristall-shining quiuer;*
> *Giue vnto the flying hart*
> *Space to breathe, how short soeuer:*
> *Thou that mak'st a day of night,*
> *Goddesse, excellently bright.*

Many words here suggest the idea of brightness (for example, '*siluer*', '*cleere*', '*pearle*', '*cristall-shining*'), but more striking is how this effect is strengthened by the refrain with its recurrent rhyme on '*bright*'. Moreover, as Trimpi points out,[3] Jonson, using the adverb '*excellently*', not only avoids more obvious words which would have stressed the sensuous quality of light, but suggests that Cynthia's brightness is an active thing working to a purpose. It is by such slight, but all-important, modifications of commonplaces that Jonson's lyrics work. The identification of Queen Elizabeth with the goddess of the moon

---

1. *Ibid.*, 80.
2. E.g. *ibid.*, 92, 161, 164, 169.
3. Trimpi, p. 207.

and of chastity was in Jonson's day the most common of common-places; but his lyric, in its conciseness, the firmness of its structure, and above all in the sharpness and clarity of its very ordinary diction, is one of his most distinguished poems.

By far the best discussion of Jonson's lyrics is that by Walker, who believes that 'Ben Jonson's originality achieves its most triumphant expression' in lyrical verse.[1] I am not so sure of the pre-eminence of Jonson's lyrical verse, which seems to me slighter than much of his other work; but Walker defines very well the quality peculiar to the lyrics:

> Emotional impulse and craftsmanship are inextricably combined in the pre-eminently successful lyrics like the *Song to Celia* or the *Hymn to Diana*. The beauty expressed in the finished lyric is a beauty which belongs to, and cannot be expressed otherwise than in craftsmanship. The conscious artistry of Ben Jonson's lyric style is a cause and a result of his poetic emotion.[2]

It is not surprising that Walton, who is concerned more with Jonson's 'social' poetry, should mock at 'the kind of seventeenth-century Mallarmé implied by Mr Ralph Walker'.[3] Passages like these two do seem to ask for that taunt:

> His lyric at its best possesses a peculiar integrity of its own, it seems to express nothing beyond or behind itself, but, in its final state, to be itself the idea which it expresses.[4]

> Ben Jonson's peculiar lyric achievement is a poetry which is, in its own way, 'absolute'.[5]

But, although Walker emphasizes this quality to the neglect of others (particularly the relevance which the lyrics often have to matters quite outside themselves), he has hit on something of great importance. In fact, before I read Walton, I had been reminded by Walker's essay of Stefan George, who was of course an admirer of Mallarmé and

---

1. Walker, pp. 181–2.
2. *Ibid.*, p. 187.
3. Walton, p. 24.
4. Walker, p. 187.
5. *Ibid.*, p. 192.

other Symbolists.[1] These lines, for instance, which are talking about themselves as much as about Maximin, have a very Jonsonian ring:

> *Du schlank und rein wie eine flamme*
> *Du wie der morgen zart und licht*
> *Du blühend reis vom edlen stamme*
> *Du wie ein quell geheim und schlicht*[2]

(You slender and pure as a flame, you like the dawn delicate and clear, you blooming branch from a noble stock, you like a secret and simple spring.)

There is at least an illuminating hint in Walker's over-simplification:

> ... there is not the normal opposition between art and inspiration – for art is its inspiration.[3]

To put it another way – to appreciate Jonson's lyrics we need to have some of the interest his contemporaries had in *jeux d'esprit*, an interest which in its extreme form enjoyed seeing how a poet could use difficult verse-forms which 'try the makers cunning'.[4] A comment like this on the Charis poems is altogether too moralistic and heavy-handed:

> In an age which can no longer attain the heroic greatness implicit in the idealized conventions of classical and Elizabethan love poetry it is better at least to be honest in asserting the ugly reality of Jacobean morality for what it is.[5]

This is much more just:

> ... the Anacreontic lightness of parts of 'A Celebration of Charis'

---

1. Stefan George, 'Franken' (1907), *Werke*, I, 1958, 235:
> '*Da schirmten held und sänger das Geheimnis:*
> *Villiers sich hoch genug für einen thron.*
> *Verlaine in fall und busse fromm und kindlich*
> *Und für sein denkbild blutend: Mallarmé.*'

(There, hero and singer shielded the Mystery: Villiers who thought himself exalted enough for a throne, Verlaine pious and childlike in his falling and repentance, and – bleeding for his monument – Mallarmé.)

2. 'Du schlank und rein wie eine flamme' (1929), *ibid.*, 469.

3. Walker, p. 192.

4. Puttenham, *op. cit.*, p. 87.

5. P.M. Cubeta, '"A Celebration of Charis"': An Evaluation of Jonsonian Poetic Strategy', *E.L.H.*, xxv, No. 3 (September 1958), 180.

is charming precisely because it fits the character which Jonson creates for himself of the old (and safe) gallant. Other attitudes are assumed, some of them doubtless 'sincere', and in all of them the tone is right for the occasion; but the artistry is almost always a result not only of aesthetic but also of temperamental 'distance'. Perhaps this combination is what one usually means by 'classical restraint'. It is a combination, at any rate, which Jonson exhibits to perfection.[1]

A poem which has the wit and lightness of touch we require from a *jeu d'esprit*, without being ultimately trivial,[2] is '*My Picture left in Scotland*'.[3] Swinburne is right, I think, when he says it is 'something more than smooth and neat'.[4] 'Jonson's muse visiting his friends in slippers'?[5] Dancing pumps would be more appropriate.

From the first we can admire the delicacy of touch, the mastery of the verse-form, and the pleasing tinkle of the rhymes in:

> *I now thinke, Love is rather deafe, then blind,*
> *For else it could not be,*
> *That she,*
> *Whom I adore so much, should so slight me,*
> *And cast my love behind . . .*

If this at first seems facile, it is worth noticing how the emphasis is made to fall on 'slight' in the fourth line. Then, as we read on, we see how the playful consideration of Cupid with which the poem opens is developed into something more profound by the end of the poem:

> *And all these through her eyes, have stopt her eares.*

The return to the idea contained in the first line is aesthetically satisfying, and the last line is a development of the first, not a mere repetition.

Similarly, the pun on 'wast' in the second section of the poem gives pleasure first by its light humour, but then leads to a line which, while even more humorous in its hyperbole, is also rather sad:

---

1. R. F. Blanchard, *op. cit.*, p. 209.
2. Contrast Herford, II, 390: '. . . little more than a *jeu d'esprit*'.
3. Herford, VIII, 149.
4. Swinburne, p. 105.
5. John Palmer, *op. cit.*, p. 226. It is plain from what Palmer says on p. 229 that he means that Jonson has taken little trouble to polish the poem.

> *Oh, but my conscious feares,*
> *That flie my thoughts betweene,*
> *Tell me that she hath seene*
> *My hundred of gray haires,*
> *Told seven and fortie years,*
> *Read so much wast, as she cannot imbrace*
> *My mountaine belly, and my rockie face,*
> *And all these through her eyes, have stopt her eares.*

Mastery of verse-form is again evident in those last few lines of the poem which are a perfect illustration of what Daniel called

> the apt planting the sentence where it may best stand to hit, the certaine close of delight with the full body of a iust period well carried...[1]

This poem is as much about Jonson the poet as about Jonson the lover: his mockery of his inadequacy as a lover is a demonstration of his skill as a poet. The poem is, as its title leads us to expect, a picture of the author's appearance and character; his love – whether it is real, or assumed for the sake of the poem, does not matter – is seen in the context of his temperament and ideals, so that even this comparatively slight poem gathers meaning as we re-read it. In the last analysis it is far from trivial.[2]

Jonson's religious lyrics are not very different in style from his secular lyrics,[3] and have been adversely criticized in a similar way. A good example is 'A Hymne to God the Father',[4] one of a group of devotional poems of which Palmer says:

> These poems of devotion are a pious exercise, of interest only as showing how even the most powerful and independent minds can honestly subscribe to doctrines without allowing them seriously to affect their conduct or vital concerns.[5]

1. Samuel Daniel, *A Defence of Ryme* (1603), *Poems and A Defence of Ryme*, ed. Arthur Colby Sprague, 1950, p. 139.
2. Cf. Trimpi, p. 234: 'There has been a genuine misunderstanding of Jonson's love poetry. It is usually called artistic, impersonal, or passionless with some condescension by those who regard the love poem solely as a form for spontaneous expression of feeling and as somehow suspect if it displays the objectivity necessary to a controlled statement.... He does not treat love in isolation but in the whole context of his experience; the increased objectivity should not be interpreted as lack of passion.'
3. Walker, p. 187; F. W. Bradbrook, *op. cit.*, p. 140.
4. Herford, VIII, 129.
5. John Palmer, *op. cit.*, p. 300.

Gregory Smith presumably means something similar when he denies the religious lyrics 'all finesse in emotion'.[1] It is true that there is something lacking from these poems which we might have expected to find in them; P. M. Cubeta explains precisely what that something is:

> One finds none of the violently dramatic power felt in Donne's 'Spit in my face you Jewes, and pierce my side . . .' or 'Batter my heart, three person'd God'. And the fluctuation between joy and despair is not so intense as it is apt to be in Donne. Jonson never manifests any sustained doubts about the possibility of his ultimate salvation. His religious poems may open with the plaintive cry of the despairing sinner, but each closes with his confidence fully restored.[2]

Jonson does indeed show towards God only a little less of the self-confidence he showed towards men. Nowadays, when it seems almost *de rigeur* for a poet who is a Christian to make it plain that he does not enjoy being one, Jonson's serenity is not likely to be popular. Here, as so often, he requires a different sort of appreciation from that which Donne requires.

The most important thing to recognize about 'A Hymne to God the Father' is that it is just that, a hymn,[3] and has the characteristics of one. It has simplicity, clarity, and dignity, and expresses beliefs and attitudes which are public rather than private, the beliefs and attitudes of all who sing it. The lucid expression of orthodox beliefs can be compelling in its own way:

> *Who more can crave*
> *Then thou hast done?*
> *That gav'st a Sonne,*
> *To free a slave,*
> *First made of nought;*
> *With all since bought.*

That may annoy by its air of having said the last word on what is, after all, a complex and debatable matter; but it is significant that

---

1. Smith, p. 238.
2. 'Ben Jonson's Religious Lyrics', *J.E.G.P.*, LXII (1963), 110.
3. Herford, XI, 49 mentions that this poem 'was used as an anthem in one of the royal chapels in and after 1653 . . .'.

other seventeenth-century poets simplify their usual styles when they write hymns: Vaughan does in 'Peace'[1] and Herbert does in 'Discipline',[2] for instance.

'Discipline' is in fact very similar, in form and in theme, to 'A Hymne to God the Father', and so is Herrick's '*An Ode, or Psalme, to God*'.[3] It is illuminating to compare these poems. Herrick, characteristically, is lighter in tone than Jonson, and even in this religious work one senses the habitual smile:

> *But since*
> *Thou didst convince*
> *My sinnes, by gently striking;*
> *Add still to those*
> *First stripes, new blowes,*
> *According to Thy liking.*

That has not the weight of this:

> *If thou hadst not*
> *Beene sterne to mee,*
> *But left me free,*
> *I had forgot*
> *My selfe and thee.*

With Herbert we see not only a difference, but a superiority to Jonson:

> *Throw away thy rod;*
> *Though man frailties hath,*
> *Thou art God:*
> *Throw away thy wrath.*

The tone of intimate humility in 'Thou art God', as of a child coaxing his father, shows a subtlety which Jonson's greater self-confidence cannot manage:

> *Heare mee, O God!*
> *A broken heart,*
> *Is my best part:*
> *Use still thy rod,*
> *That I may prove*
> *Therein, thy Love.*

1. *Poetry and Selected Prose*, ed. L. C. Martin, 1963, p. 261.
2. *The Works of George Herbert*, ed. F. E. Hutchinson, 1941, reprinted 1945, p. 178.
3. *The Poems of Robert Herrick*, ed. L. C. Martin, 1965, p. 363.

One feels that the rod is rather more necessary in Jonson's case.

It is fair to say that Jonson cannot match Herbert on Herbert's own ground, or indeed match Vaughan whose 'Peace' shows, like Herbert's poem, a power of condensing strong religious aspiration into the simplest words:

> *If thou canst get but thither,*
> *There growes the flowre of peace . . .*[1]

Here the specialists are superior to the virtuoso.

Jonson's virtuosity in the lyric can be seen from '*A Fit of Rime against Rime*'.[2] This is certainly not about love or religion, or any of those subjects naturally associated with the lyric, although there has been some uncertainty as to what it *is* about. George Hemphill has suggested that by 'rime' Jonson does not mean 'consonance of terminal sounds in words or lines' but 'all the conventions of verse, particularly the modern ones'.[3] I suggest that Hemphill is wrong, and that when we investigate what Jonson does mean by 'rime' we see that this poem, which is primarily a joke, is a joke that loses much of its point if we do not take the word 'rime' in its modern sense, and also that there is a serious controversy behind the joke.

The title, with its pun on '*Fit*' (a section of a poem and a paroxysm) and its indication of the paradox that lies behind the whole poem ('*Rime against Rime*'), warns us that we should not read the poem too gravely – which does not mean that we cannot take it seriously. A further paradox is that the verse-form Jonson uses here is intended to draw attention to the rhyming and to demonstrate how rhyme 'expresseth but by fits', even while our knowledge that Jonson is doing this deliberately makes us aware both of his skill and of the poem's dependence on the abused rhyme for much of its effect:

> *Rime, the rack of finest wits,*
> *That expresseth but by fits,*
> > *True Conceipt,*
> *Spoyling Senses of their Treasure,*
> *Cosening Judgement with a measure,*
> > *But false weight.*

---

1. *Loc. cit.*, p. 148 above.

2. Herford, VIII, 183.

3. George Hemphill, 'Jonson's "Fit of Rime Against Rime"', *Explicator*, XII, No. 8 (June 1954), Article 50.

It is illuminating to see the origins of the two meanings which the word 'rime' could have:

> In med. Latin *rithmi, rithmici versus*, were used to denote the more popular accentual versifying in contrast to the more learned quantitative verse. Common use of similar sounding endings in *rithmi* led to the use of *rime* (later *rhyme*) as the general term for compositions with this particular feature.[1]

This leads us naturally to the famous controversy between Campion and Daniel, which probably occasioned Jonson's poem. The main bone of contention was what Campion described contemptuously as

> that which ends in the like sound, so that verses in such manner composed yeeld but a continual repetition of that Rhetoricall figure which we tearme *similiter desinentia*, and that, being but *figura verbi*, ought (as *Tully* and all other Rhetoricians have iudicially obseru'd) sparingly to be vs'd...[2]

and what Daniel described reverently as

> an agreeing sound in the last silables of seuerall verses, giuing both to the Eare an Eccho of a delightfull report & to the Memorie a deeper impression of what is deliuered therein.[3]

Jonson was of course interested in this, as in every other, controversy, and he told Drummond

> he had written a discourse of Poesie both against Campion & Daniel especially this Last, wher he proves couplets to be the bravest sort of Verses, especially when they are broken, like Hexameters and that crosse Rimes and Stanzaes (becaus the pūrpose would lead him beyond 8 lines to conclude) were all forced.[4]

One would expect Jonson to disagree with Campion's advocacy of quantitative measures in English, for all Jonson's practice is against this sort of classicism; but it is not so easy to see why he disagreed

---

1. Editorial note in Sir Philip Sidney, *An Apology for Poetry*, ed. Geoffrey Shepherd, 1965, p. 233. Sidney, writing at some time between 1579 and 1586, uses the word in its modern sense, *ibid.*, p. 140: '... that like sounding of the words, which we call rhyme.'

2. *Observations in the Art of English Poesie* (1602), *Campion's Works*, ed. Percival Vivian, 1909, p. 36.

3. *A Defence of Ryme* (1603), *op. cit.*, p. 132.

4. *Conversations*, Herford, I, 132.

with Daniel. Of course he enjoyed disagreeing with anyone; but there is more to it than that. Jonson's remarks to Drummond suggest two reasons. Jonson's favourite form, 'couplets . . . the bravest sort of Verses', had been spoken of slightingly by Daniel:

> . . . I must confesse, that to mine owne eare, those continuall cadences of couplets vsed in long and continued Poemes, are very tyresome, and vnpleasing, by reason that still, me thinks, they runne on with a sound of one nature, and a kinde of certaintie which stuffs the delight rather then intertaines it.[1]

Moreover, Daniel had expressed a preference above all for 'alternate or cross Ryme'[2] and particularly mentioned stanzas of six, seven, and eight lines.[3]

Jonson's 'discourse of Poesie' is not extant; but '*A Fit of Rime against Rime*' contains much evidence that it too was occasioned by Daniel's *Defence of Ryme*. Some of Daniel's most telling arguments in favour of rhyme are disagreed with so definitely by Jonson that it is very possible that allusions to Daniel's treatise are intended:

> *Soone as lazie thou wert knowne,*
> *All good Poëtrie hence was flowne,*
> > *And Art banish'd.*
> *For a thousand yeares together,*
> *All Parnassus Greene did wither,*
> > *And wit vanish'd.*

The apostrophe 'lazie thou' reads like a reply to Daniel's suggestion that the need for rhyme may even help a poet, a suggestion which – however acute and often true – must have annoyed the man who prided himself on writing all his poems first in prose:

> . . . sure in an eminent spirit whome Nature hath fitted for that mysterie, Ryme is no impediment to his conceit, but rather giues him wings to mount and carries him, not out of his course, but as it were beyond his power to a farre happier flight. Al excellencies being sold vs at the hard price of labour, it followes, where we bestow most thereof, we buy the best successe: and Ryme being

---

1. *Ibid.*, p. 155
2. *Ibid.*, p. 156.
3. *Ibid.*, pp. 138–9.

farre more laborious then loose measures (whatsoeuer is obiected) must needs, meeting with wit and industry, breed greater and worthier effects in our language.[1]

Daniel's contention that the need for rhyme carries 'an eminent spirit . . . not out of his course' has already been denied by Jonson's description of rhyme as

Wresting words, from their true calling.

Then Jonson's statement:

> *For a thousand yeares together,*
> *All* Parnassus *Greene did wither,*

reads like a humorous rebuttal of this:

> . . . is it not a most apparant ignorance, both of the succession of learning in *Europe*, and the generall course of things, *to say, that all lay pittifully deformed in those lacke-learning times from the declining of the Romane Empire, till the light of the Latin tongue was reuiued by* Rewcline, Erasmus *and* Moore.[2]

Even the phrase '*the light of the Latin tongue*' is echoed by Jonson in 'All light failed!'

Jonson has what seem to be verbal echoes of Daniel elsewhere in his poem; none of these apparent echoes is by itself distinctive enough for us to be sure that Jonson intends an allusion, but the cumulative effect is persuasive. 'Joynting Syllabes', by which I take Jonson to mean breaking a word for the sake of a rhyme,[3] is reminiscent of Daniel's complaint against Campion's arrogance:

> For who hath constituted him to be the *Radamanthus* thus to torture sillables . . .[4]

and his complaint that classical Latin verse, in its need to observe quantity, resulted in

> torturing and dismembring of wordes in the middest, or disioyning

---

1. *Ibid.*, pp. 137–8.
2. *Ibid.*, p. 140. Daniel is here referring to Campion, *op. cit.*, p. 35.
3. As he does sometimes himself, e.g. Herford, VIII, 211, lines 183–4; *ibid.*, 305, lines 20–1.
4. *Op. cit.*, p. 149.

such as naturally should be married and march together, by setting them as far asunder, as they can possibly stand . . .[1]

A fault that Daniel says is incident to quantity is thus said by Jonson to be incident to rhyme. Similarly Daniel's suggestion that words in quantitative measure tend to 'fall downe into flatte prose'[2] is turned by Jonson into a complaint against rhyme:

> *Propping Verse, for feare of falling*
> > *To the ground.*

Another complaint of Jonson's against rhyme is that it is

> *Fastning Vowells, as with fetters*
> > *They were bound!*

Daniel used the same terms to suggest that, if Campion's suggestions were adopted and rhyme discarded, poets would merely 'put off these fetters to receiue others'.[3] Then Daniel refers to Campion as a 'tyrant',[4] and Jonson refers to '*Tyran* Rime'. Finally, although here we are of course dealing with a proverbial phrase, where Daniel says:

as good still to vse rhyme and a little reason, as neither ryme nor reason,[5]

Jonson says:

> *Stil may reason warre with rime,*
> > *Resting never.*

It seems to me, then, that this poem is partly a humorous paradox – rhyme attacking rhyme – and partly a joke at the expense of Daniel. The joke is a good-natured one, and indeed my final impression is that Jonson's main implication here is that the Campion–Daniel controversy was not good for anything but a joke.[6] The comic curse at the end of the poem, with its pun on 'feet', is in Jonson's best light manner:

---

1. *Ibid.*, pp. 136–7.
2. *Ibid.*, p. 137.
3. *Ibid.*, p. 135.
4. *Ibid.*, p. 149.
5. *Ibid.*, p. 135.
6. This is not to imply that his lost 'discourse of Poesie' (see above, p. 150) did not treat the matter seriously.

> *He that first invented thee,*
> *May his joynts tormented bee,*
>> *Cramp'd for ever;*
> *Still may Syllabes jarre with time,*
> *Stil may reason warre with rime,*
>> *Resting never.*
> *May his Sense, when it would meet*
> *The cold tumor in his feet,*
>> *Grow unsounder.*
> *And his Title be long foole,*
> *That in rearing such a Schoole,*
>> *Was the founder.*

If some of the best of Jonson's lyrics are in a sense 'occasional' poems – not merely exercises in style (although they are that too), but also poems with great relevance to matters outside themselves – then this is even more true of the best of his odes.[1] 'Where do'st thou careless lie',[2] for instance, shows the same mastery of verse-form as his best lyrics, so that we can hardly imagine the content in any other form, and the same use of the verse-form to stress meaning and tone. Most striking is how each stanza leads up to a long last line which never seems a mere addition but always the inevitable culmination of what has gone before:

> *Where do'st thou careless lie,*
> *Buried in ease and sloth?*
> *Knowledge, that sleepes, doth die;*
> *And this Securitie,*
>> *It is the common Moath,*
> *That eats on wits, and Arts and ⟨oft⟩ destroyes them both.*

There is the *élan*, the singing power, we expect from an ode. At the same time there are qualities similar to those found in Jonson's poems in couplets. There is the customary air of self-sufficiency and stoicism:

> *Minds that are great and free,*
> *Should not on fortune pause,*
> *'Tis crowne enough to vertue still, her owne applause.*

---

1. E.g. '*Ode:*' ('Yff Men and tymes were nowe'), Herford, VIII, 419, and the two odes to himself, *ibid.*, 174, and Herford, VI, 492.
2. '*An Ode. To himselfe*', Herford, VIII, 174.

Moreover, this poem, which is not only '*To himselfe*' but also largely about himself, is not without social reference. Gnomic utterances like

> *Knowledge, that sleepes, doth die*

clearly have a general relevance. The typical contrast that runs throughout, between the skilled poet on the one hand and unskilled versifiers and incompetent readers on the other, is not mere arrogance; it is justified by the artistry which his poem reveals:

> *What though the greedie Frie*
> *Be taken with false Baytes*
> *Of worded Balladrie,*
> *And thinke it Poësie?*
> *They die with their conceits,*
> *And only pitious scorne, upon their folly waites.*

The elevated style suitable to an ode is attained, typically, with the homeliest diction,[1] while a blend of homely imagery[2] and classical reference emphasizes the general nature of what Jonson is saying, and establishes his right to speak for all true poets:

> *Are all th' Aonian springs*
> *Dri'd up? lyes Thespia wast?*
> *Doth Clarius Harp want strings,*
> *That not a Nymph now sings?*
> *Or droop they as disgrac't,*
> *To see their Seats and Bowers by chattring Pies defac't?*

Although each stanza is powerful in itself and comes to a climax in its last line, the thought also progresses throughout the poem; the major climax is in the last stanza where, despite the fact that its origins are in personal disappointment (and there is no attempt to disguise this), the authority with which it speaks is more than personal and the enemies of that authority become generalized in images which embody malignity and stupidity with clarity and force:

---

1. Trimpi, pp. 200–1: 'The emotional intensity of the three odes that Jonson wrote to himself sometimes makes it difficult to see that they owe their essential power to the qualities of the plain style.'

2. Leavis, *op. cit.*, footnote to p. 22 quotes the first stanza of the poem I am discussing to show 'the kind of imagery that, going with Jonson's idiomatic manner, helps him, as an influence, to blend so easily with Donne'.

And since our Daintie age,
Cannot indure reproofe,
Make not thy selfe a Page,
To that strumpet the Stage,
But sing high and aloofe,
Safe from the wolves black jaw, and the dull Asses hoofe.

Of course, we shall not like even '*An Ode. To himselfe*' if we dislike the expression of pride and scorn. In this, I find Jonson very similar to Yeats[1] who also has won the admiration of many who dislike his attitudes:

Time that with this strange excuse
Pardoned Kipling and his views,
And will pardon Paul Claudel,
Pardons him for writing well.[2]

The 'Lyrick sweetnesse'[3] of Jonson lies in the total effect of the finished product which is often made from materials which in their raw state are far from sweet.

Moreover, even in his lyrics and odes Jonson can hardly be said to lift his readers up from the earth to give them a view of other worlds; rather he forces us to look more closely at the world in which we live, and often at its most dingy features:

... our dislike of romantic excesses, such as the embarrassing parts of Wordsworth's ode, still leaves unharmed the great poetry of Jonson's own and slightly later days, from 'Full fathom five' to 'The Retreat', and of these worlds the clear-eyed, robust, concrete Jonson has at most partial glimpses.[4]

The comparisons made here indicate, not faults, but limitations to Jonson's power as a poet. A recognition of these limitations should suggest what is his peculiar strength:

Jonson saw all life without mystery or cause for reverence; full of clear detail, a definite matter that could be shaped by any brain and will that were strong enough.[5]

1. F. W. Bradbrook, *op. cit.*, p. 140. See also Appendix B, p. 161.

2. W.H. Auden, 'In Memory of W.B.Yeats', *Another Time*, 1940, fifth impression 1946, p. 109.

3. Above, p. 134.

4. Douglas Bush, *English Literature in the Earlier Seventeenth Century 1600–1660*, p. 111.

5. Anon, 'The Triumph of Ben Jonson. Tests of Poetic Magic', *T.L.S.*, 4 July 1936, p. 550.

This is hardly just. There is reverence in Jonson's poetry – for friendship, honesty, and above all for 'any brain and will that were strong enough'. Yet, while his capacity for friendship is attractive, his glorification (often overt, and nearly always at least implicit in his manner) of poetic skill probably has less appeal for most readers. We do get glimpses of a Jonson who inspires affection, as in this remark to Drummond:

> he heth consumed a whole night jn looking to his great toe, about which he hath seen tartars & turks Romans and Carthaginions feight in his jmagination.[1]

But in his poetry, even his playfulness is so skilled and professional that it occasions admiration more readily than affection. Nor does he give the impression of wanting affection. There is no easy way into his poetry, and he did not intend that there should be; to read him with enjoyment requires great care and attention,

As if there were no saboath of the minde.[2]

Jonson is certainly a very varied poet but, behind all the variety, we sense the same personality which, while it attracts some today as it did many in his lifetime, still manages to repel many others. That personality is itself varied – sometimes stern, sometimes playful, always honest and often brusque – but my dominant impression is of a man who was above all a poet, and a poet who deserves, if not love, at least great admiration for poems which

> *Give cause to some of wonnder, some despite,*
> *But vnto more dispayre to Imitate their sounde.*[3]

---

1. *Conversations*, Herford, I, 141.
2. Samuel Daniel, 'To the Reader', *op. cit.*, p. 3.
3. '*Ode:*', Herford, VIII, 420.

APPENDIX A

An Outline of Jonson's Life[1]

Ben Jonson was born in 1572, probably in or near London, the post-humous son of a clergyman. Within three years his mother was married again, this time to a master-bricklayer of Westminster.

Jonson attended Westminster School and was taught by the famous scholar and antiquary William Camden to whom he later expressed his gratitude in *Epigrammes*, XIIII (p. 31).

After leaving school, Jonson worked for a time, probably at brick-laying. In later life his enemies frequently taunted him with this early occupation.

He served as a soldier in the Low Countries where, finding the fighting at a standstill, he challenged an enemy to single combat and killed him. He boasted of his military experience in *Epigrammes*, CVIII (p. 69).

Back in England, Jonson spent some time acting in a strolling company, apparently with little success. By July 1597 he was employed by Henslowe as a playwright. In 1598 *Every Man in his Humour* was performed by the Lord Chamberlain's Company at the Curtain. Shakespeare took a leading role in the performance, and there is a tradition that he recommended the play to this Company. A few days after the performance, Jonson fought and killed the actor Gabriel Spencer in a duel. He was arrested, and escaped hanging only by pleading benefit of clergy; his goods were confiscated, and his thumb was branded.

While in prison, Jonson was converted to Roman Catholicism by a priest who was also a prisoner. He remained a Catholic for eleven years, and then was reconciled to the Anglican Church.

In 1600 *Cynthia's Revels* was acted by the Boys of the Chapel Royal. In 1601 *Poetaster* was acted by the same Company; this play was Jonson's contribution to the 'War of the Theatres' in which his principal opponents were Marston and Dekker.

1. All the page-references are to Herford, VIII.

From 1602 to 1607 Jonson lived in the household of Esmé Stewart, Lord Aubigny, to whom he addressed *Epigrammes*, CXXVII (p. 80). *The Forrest*, XIII (p. 116) was written to Aubigny's wife.

Jonson had married in 1594. The death of his son Benjamin in 1603, at the age of seven, occasioned one of his most famous elegies, *Epigrammes*, XLV (p. 41). Another child, a daughter who died at six months, is commemorated in *Epigrammes*, XXII (p. 33).

In 1603 Jonson wrote his first 'entertainments' for the new King, James I. Between 1605 and 1631 Jonson wrote many masques for presentation at Court. It was probably in 1612 that he first quarrelled with his collaborator in the masques, Inigo Jones, whom he attacked many times in his poetry (pp. 62, 74, 81, 402, 406, 407).

The Gunpowder Plot of 1605 is alluded to in *Epigrammes*, LX (p. 46) which was written to Lord Mounteagle, a Catholic who helped to reveal the Plot.

Volpone was acted in 1606, *The Alchemist* in 1610, and *Bartholomew Fair* in 1614.

1616 saw the publication of the *Works* in folio; this contains *Epigrammes* and *The Forrest*, but nothing written later than 1612.

In 1618–9 Jonson walked to Scotland where he visited the poet Drummond of Hawthornden who kept a record of Jonson's remarks. This record is valuable for the details it gives of Jonson's life, and still more for the impression it gives of his personality. '*The Houre-glasse*' (p. 148) is quoted by Drummond, and '*My Picture left in* Scotland' (p. 149) was sent to Drummond after Jonson had left.

Jonson's house burned down in 1623 and many of his manuscripts were destroyed; see '*An Execration upon Vulcan*' (p. 202). In the same year Jonson contributed two poems to the Shakespeare Folio (p. 390).

From about 1616 to the death of James in 1625, Jonson's reputation was very high. He presided at famous meetings of friends and disciples at various taverns – the Sun, the Dog, the Triple Tun, and the Old Devil (where the upper chamber they used was known as the 'Apollo'). Admission to the 'Tribe of Ben' was clearly an honour (see p. 218), and among the 'Sons of Ben', as they were sometimes called, were Carew and Herrick.

Jonson's *Discoveries*, a work of criticism, much of it translation or adaptation of other authors but still valuable for its insight into Jonson's own critical attitudes, was probably written after the death of James.

During the reign of Charles Jonson lost much of his prestige at Court and was often in want. He was paralysed by a stroke in 1628; see '*An Epistle Mendicant*' (p. 248) and '*An Epigram, To the House-hold*' (p. 241). His return to the stage in 1629 with *The New Inn* was a fiasco; nevertheless, the ode 'Come leave the lothed Stage' (included, when the play was published, as a counter-attack to critics of the play) shows his powers as a non-dramatic poet were at their height.

Jonson died in 1637 and was buried in Westminster Abbey. The inscription 'O rare Ben Jonson' marks his grave.

In 1640–1 the *Works* (two folio volumes) were published by Sir Kenelm Digby.

Jonson and Yeats

It comes as something of a surprise to meet, in the middle of one of Jonson's epistles, a couplet with such a Yeatsian ring as this:

> *The Servant of the Serving-woman, in scorne,*
> *Ne're came to taste the plenteous Mariage-horne.*[1]

The very feel of this reminds us of Yeats, while 'the plenteous Mariage-horne' can hardly fail to bring 'A Prayer for my Daughter'[2] to mind.

We know from Yeats's letters that he had read Jonson's masques and had a very high opinion of some of the plays.[3] There is also one occasion in Yeats's poems when he admits a debt to Jonson:

> *... surmise companions*
> *Beyond the fling of the dull ass's hoof*
> *—Ben Jonson's phrase—...*[4]

Yeats may well have taken the phrase from '*An Ode. To himselfe*',[5] although it is perhaps more likely that he took it from the 'apologeticall Dialogue' at the end of *Poetaster*[6] which he had certainly read.[7]

Another parallel, which may be a reminiscence of Jonson by Yeats, is this:

> *Yet would be now, could I but have my wish,*
> *Colder and dumber and deafer than a fish.*[8]

---

1. '*An Epistle to a Friend, to perswade him to the Warres*', Herford, VIII, 165.
2. *Collected Poems*, p. 211.
3. *The Letters of W.B. Yeats*, ed. Allan Wade, 1954, pp. 450, 478, 479, 664, 671.
4. '*While I, from that reed-throated whisperer*', *Collected Poems*, p. 143.
5. Herford, VIII, 175.
6. Herford. IV, 324.
7. *Letters*, p. 479.
8. 'All Things can Tempt me', *Collected Poems*, p. 109.

> *Last, in the fishes place, sits he, doth say;*
> In married ioyes, all should be dumbe, as they.[1]

Lastly, this:

> *I made my song a coat*
> *Covered with embroideries*
> *Out of old mythologies*
> *From heel to throat;*
> *But the fools caught it ...*[2]

sounds to me as though it were suggested by this:

> *Yff Men, and tymes were nowe*
>   *Of that true fface*
> *As when they both were greate, and both knewe howe*
>   *that ffortune to imbrace,*
> *By Cherissheinge the Spirrites yt gaue their greatnesse grace:*
> *I then could rayse my notes*
> *Lowd to the wondringe thronge*
> *And better Blason them, then all their Coates,*
> *That were the happie subiect of my songe.*[3]

The two passages are similar in their pride and scorn, and in the connection which they both make between 'Coates' and 'songe'. The different meanings of 'coat' in the two passages (garment in Yeats and heraldic coat in Jonson) suggest that the borrowing, if there was one, was largely a recollection of the sound. It may be of significance that Yeats's poem was first published within a few months of *'While I, from that reed-throated whisperer'*[4] which admits to a reminiscence of Jonson.

---

1. *The Haddington Masque*, Herford, VII, 259. Jonson is probably remembering Horace, *Odes* iv. 3 (Loeb edition, p. 292):

> *o mutis quoque piscibus*
>   *donatura cycni, si libeat, sonum ...*

(*O you who, if you wanted, could also give the voice of a swan to dumb fishes ...*)
It is possible that Yeats also drew directly from Horace.

2. 'A Coat', *Collected Poems*, p. 142.

3. '*Ode:*', Herford, VIII, 419.

4. 'A Coat' was published first in May 1914 and *'While I, from that reed-throated whisperer'* in February 1914; see *The Variorum Edition of the Poems of W.B. Yeats*, ed. Peter Allt and Russell K. Alspach, p. 320.

APPENDIX C

A Jonsonian Crux

One of Jonson's lyrics is notable for obscurity of a kind we do not expect from him. What meaning are we to take from the last two lines here?

> *The thirst, that from the soule doth rise,*
> *Doth aske a drinke diuine:*
> *But might I of Ioue's Nectar sup,*
> *I would not change for thine.*[1]

John Press comments that these lines

appear to contradict the meaning which he presumably intended and, despite William Empson's ingenious explanation of the passage, I still do not know whether Jonson is being remarkably subtle or unusually careless.[2]

Empson, to whom this is an example of ambiguity 'irrelevant to the total effect intended'[3] and 'a puzzling example',[4] says:

This is not to say that the last two lines are an accident, and should be altered; you may feel it gives a touching completeness to his fervour that he feels so sure no one will misunderstand him.[5]

I do not find this convincing. If these two lines do 'say the opposite of what is meant',[6] then Jonson is being 'unusually careless'.

There have, of course, been other attempts to provide a solution. Gerald Bullett suggested that 'for' was a printer's error for 'fro' or 'from'.[7] E. A. Horsman replied that 'for' was a well-authenticated reading, and he made another suggestion:

---

1. '*Song*. To Celia', Herford, VIII, 106.
2. *The Chequer'd Shade*, 1958, p. 17.
3. *Seven Types of Ambiguity*, 1930, quoted from Peregrine edition 1961, p. 242.
4. *Ibid.*
5. *Ibid.*
6. *Ibid.*
7. Letter to *T.L.S.*, 1 June 1956, p. 329.

    ... *change* is commonly used in the seventeenth century where we would use *exchange*, and Jonson is saying that he would not exchange for Celia's cup (with the kiss in it) even Jove's nectar.[1]

This solves nothing, for Jonson is still saying what he should not be saying, except that Horsman does not seem aware of it any longer.

    Marshall Van Deusen mentions how the *O.E.D.* fails to provide a suitable meaning for 'change'.[2] Then he reports an intriguing suggestion by Yvor Winters that Jonson means: 'Only if I might drink of Jove's nectar, would I not change for (that is, would I refuse) thine'.[3] Unfortunately, this is a meaning which disrupts the tone of the poem as a whole in which, as Empson says, 'a simple lyrism is intended'.[4] Other suggestions that Van Deusen mentions are totally unconvincing.[5]

    We are still left with the problem that Jonson has not apparently made himself clear; and clarity is one of the outstanding features of his lyrics. If we could find an appropriate meaning for 'change', the difficulty would disappear. I think there is such a meaning and some support for it from a near-contemporary source.

> *Is this the Region, this the Soil, the Clime,*
> *Said then the lost Arch-Angel, this the seat*
> *That we must change for Heav'n, this mournful gloom*
> *For that celestial light?*[6]

As F. T. Prince says, 'change' here means 'take in exchange'.[7] With Milton's example, it seems that we have good authority for such a usage, and Jonson's lines may then be paraphrased thus: 'But even if I might sup of Jove's nectar, I would not take it in exchange for thine'. There is the difference that Milton is using 'change' transitively (with the objects 'Region', 'Soil', 'Clime', 'seat', and 'gloom'), while Jonson is using it intransitively, so that I have had to supply an object ('it') in my paraphrase. Nevertheless, this is a possible solution to the problem.

1. Letter to *T.L.S.*, 8 June 1956, p. 345.
2. 'Criticism and Ben Jonson's "To Celia"', *E.C.*, VII (1957), 97–9.
3. *Ibid.*, 99.
4. *Op. cit.*, p. 242.
5. *Op. cit.*, pp. 99–103.
6. *Paradise Lost*, Book I, lines 242–5, Milton, *Poetical Works*, ed. Helen Darbishire, I, 1952, 11.
7. *Paradise Lost Books I and II*, ed. F. T. Prince, 1962, footnote on p. 37.

Bibliography

Where more than one date is mentioned, the later date is that of the edition used.

1 EDITIONS OF JONSON AND ANTHOLOGIES CONTAINING POEMS BY HIM

Robert Bell, ed. *Poetical Works of Ben Jonson*. 1856.
Francis Cunningham, ed. *The Works of Ben Jonson*. In 3 vols. 1871.
Ronald Duncan, ed. *Selected Poems of Ben Jonson*. 1949.
C. H. Herford and Percy Simpson, eds. (with, from 1938, Evelyn Simpson). *Ben Jonson*. In 11 vols. 1925–52.
Selected by John Hollander. *Ben Jonson*. 1961.
William B. Hunter, ed. *The Complete Poetry of Ben Jonson*. 1963.
Maurice Hussey, ed. *Jonson and the Cavaliers*. 1964.
G. B. Johnston, ed. *Poems of Ben Jonson*. 1954.
Hugh Kenner, ed. *Seventeenth Century Poetry, The Schools of Donne and Jonson*. 1964.
Bernard H. Newdigate, ed. *The Poems of Ben Jonson*. 1936.

2 CRITICAL STUDIES OF JONSON

J. B. Bamborough. *Ben Jonson*. 1959.
Jonas A. Barish, ed. *Ben Jonson, A Collection of Critical Essays*. 1963.
Maurice Castelain. *Ben Jonson, L'Homme et l'Œuvre*. 1907.
Esther C. Dunn. *Ben Jonson's Art: Elizabethan Life and Literature as Reflected Therein*. 1963 (copyright 1925).
G. B. Johnston. *Ben Jonson: Poet*. 1945.
John Palmer. *Ben Jonson*. 1934.
Edward B. Partridge. *The Broken Compass, A Study of the Major Comedies of Ben Jonson*. 1958.
G. Gregory Smith. *Ben Jonson*. 1919.
A. C. Swinburne. *A Study of Ben Jonson*. 1889.
J. Addington Symonds. *Ben Jonson*. 1886.

Wesley Trimpi. *Ben Jonson's Poems. A Study of the Plain Style*. 1962.
C. F. Wheeler. *Classical Mythology in the Plays, Masques, and Poems of Ben Jonson*. 1938.

3   ESSAYS AND ARTICLES IN PERIODICALS

Anon. *The Triumph of Ben Jonson. Tests of Poetic Magic*, Times Literary Supplement, 4 July 1936.
Howard S. Babb. *The 'Epitaph on Elizabeth, L. H.' and Ben Jonson's Style*, Journal of English and Germanic Philology, LXII, 1963.
Jonas A. Barish. Review of Trimpi, *Modern Philology*, LXI, No. 3, February 1962.
Rufus A. Blanchard. *Carew and Jonson*, Studies in Philology, LII, 1955.
F. W. Bradbrook. *Ben Jonson's Poetry*, A Guide to English Literature, III, From Donne to Marvell, Boris Ford, ed. 1956.
W. D. Briggs. *Source-Material for Jonson's 'Epigrams' and 'Forest'*, Classical Philology, XI, January–October 1916.
A. D. Fitton Brown. *Drink to me, Celia*, The Modern Language Review, LIV, 1959.
Gerald Bullett. Letter to Times Literary Supplement, 1 June 1956.
Paul M. Cubeta. *A Jonsonian Ideal: 'To Penshurst'*, Philological Quarterly, XLII, No. 1, January 1963.
Paul M. Cubeta. *'A Celebration of Charis': An Evaluation of Jonsonian Poetic Strategy*, English Literary History, XXV, No. 3, September 1958.
Paul M. Cubeta. *Ben Jonson's Religious Lyrics*, Journal of English and Germanic Philology, LXII, 1963.
John F. M. Dovaston. Letter to The Monthly Magazine, XXXIX, March 1815.
J. W. Hebel. *Draytons Sirena*, Publications of the Modern Language Association, XXXIX, 1924.
George Hemphill. *Jonson's 'Fit of Rime Against Rime'*, Explicator, XII, No. 8, June 1954.
E. A. Horsman. Letter to Times Literary Supplement, 8 June 1956.
G. A. E. Parfitt. *The Poetry of Ben Jonson*, Essays in Criticism, XVIII, No. 1, January 1968.
Evelyn Simpson. *A Question of Authorship*, Review of English Studies, XV, 1939.

Ernest W. Talbert. *New Light on Ben Jonson's Workmanship*, Studies in Philology, XL, 1943.

Marshall Van Deusen. *Criticism and Ben Jonson's 'To Celia'*, Essays in Criticism, VII, 1957.

R. S. Walker. *Ben Jonson's Lyric Poetry*, Seventeenth-Century English Poetry, W. R. Keast, ed. 1962, previously published in Criterion, XIII, 1933–4.

Geoffrey Walton. *The Tone of Ben Jonson's Poetry*, Metaphysical to Augustan. Studies in Tone and Sensibility in the Seventeenth Century, 1955.

Malcolm L. Wilder. *Did Jonson write 'The Expostulation' attributed to Donne?*, Modern Language Review, XXI, 1926.

Edmund Wilson. *Morose Ben Jonson*, Ben Jonson. A Collection of Critical Essays, Jonas A. Barish, ed. 1963, previously published in The Triple Thinkers, 1938.

Yvor Winters. *The Sixteenth Century Lyric in England*, an essay in three parts, Poetry (Chicago), February, March, April 1939.

4 OTHER WORKS

Anon. *Beowulf*, translated by David Wright. 1957.

W. H. Auden. *About the House*. 1966.

W. H. Auden. *Another Time*. 1940, fifth impression 1946.

W. H. Auden. *New Year Letter*. 1941, third impression 1946.

W. H. Auden. *The Shield of Achilles*. 1955.

Geoffrey Brereton, ed. *The Penguin Book of French Verse*, vol. II. 1958.

Douglas Bush. *Classical Influences in Renaissance Literature*. 1952.

Douglas Bush. *English Literature in the Earlier Seventeenth Century 1600–1660*. 1945.

Douglas Bush. *Mythology and the Renaissance Tradition in English Poetry*. 1932.

John Buxton. *Sir Philip Sidney and the English Renaissance*. 1954.

Thomas Campion. *Campion's Works*, Percival Vivian, ed. 1909.

Thomas Carew. *The Poems of Thomas Carew with his Masque Coelum Britannicum*, Rhodes Dunlap, ed. 1949.

Catullus. *Catullus, Tibullus, and Pervigilium Veneris*, Loeb edition. 1913.

Marchette Chute. *Ben Jonson of Westminster*. 1954.

B. C. Clough. *The Metaphysical Poets*, unpublished. 1920.

Hardin Craig. *The Enchanted Glass, The Elizabethan Mind in Literature.* 1936.

Samuel Daniel. *Poems and A Defence of Ryme*, A. C. Sprague, ed. 1950.

Donald Davie. *Articulate Energy – An Enquiry into the Syntax of English Poetry.* 1955.

Donald Davie. *Purity of Diction in English Verse.* 1952.

John Donne. *The Elegies and the Songs and Sonnets of John Donne*, Helen Gardner, ed. 1965.

John Donne. *The Poems of John Donne*, H. J. C. Grierson, ed. in 2 vols. Vol. I 1912, reprinted 1938.

John Dryden. *The Poems of John Dryden*, James Kinsley, ed. in 4 vols. Vol. I 1958.

T. S. Eliot. *On Poetry and Poets.* 1957.

T. S. Eliot. *Selected Essays.* Third edition. 1951.

William Empson. *Seven Types of Ambiguity.* 1930, Peregrine edition 1961.

Stefan George. *Werke*, in 2 vols. Vol. I 1958.

Edmund Gosse. *The Jacobean Poets.* 1899.

Robert Graves. *The Greek Myths*, in 2 vols. 1955.

Sir John Harington. *A New Discourse of a Stale Subject Called the Metamorphosis of Ajax*, Elizabeth S. Donno, ed. 1962.

George Herbert. *The Works of George Herbert*, F. E. Hutchinson, ed. 1941, reprinted 1945.

Robert Herrick. *The Poems of Robert Herrick*, L. C. Martin, ed. 1965.

Gilbert Highet. *The Anatomy of Satire.* 1962.

Gilbert Highet. *The Classical Tradition. Greek and Roman Influences on Western Literature.* 1949, reprinted 1951.

Homer. *The Odyssey*, translated by E. V. Rieu. 1946, reprinted 1964.

Horace. *Odes and Epodes*, Loeb edition. 1964.

Horace. *Satires, Epistles and Ars Poetica*, Loeb edition. 1926.

A. E. Housman. *The Name and Nature of Poetry.* 1933, reprinted 1945.

A. N. Jeffares. *W. B. Yeats, Man and Poet.* 1949.

Samuel Johnson. *The Poems of Samuel Johnson*, D. Nichol Smith and E. L. McAdam, eds. 1941, reprinted 1962.

F. R. Leavis. *Revaluation.* 1936.

Laurence Lerner. *The Truest Poetry. An Essay on the Question What is Literature?* 1960.

C. Day Lewis. *The Poetic Image*. 1947.

C. S. Lewis. *English Literature in the Sixteenth Century Excluding Drama*, Vol. III of *Oxford History of English Literature*. 1954, reprinted 1962.

Robert Lynd. *Books and Writers*. 1952.

Maud Gonne MacBride. *A Servant of the Queen*. 1938.

T. T. Macan and E. B. Worthington. *Life in Lakes and Rivers*. 1951, reprinted 1962.

Kathryn A. McEuen. *Classical Influence upon the Tribe of Ben*. 1939.

S. Mallarmé. *Poésies de Stéphane Mallarmé*, Librairie Gallimard. 1945.

Andrew Marvell. *The Poems and Letters of Andrew Marvell*, H. M. Margoliouth, ed. in 2 vols. Vol. I 1927.

H. A. Mason. *Humanism and Poetry in the Early Tudor Period*. 1959.

John Milton. *Paradise Lost Books I and II*, F. T. Prince, ed. 1962.

John Milton. *Poetical Works*, Helen Darbishire, ed. in 2 vols. Vol. I 1952, Vol. II 1955.

Kenneth Muir. 'Changing Interpretations of Shakespeare', *A Guide to English Literature*, II, *The Age of Shakespeare*, Boris Ford, ed. 1955.

Sylvia Plath. *Ariel*. 1965.

Alexander Pope. *The Poems of Alexander Pope*, John Butt, ed. 1963.

Alexander Pope. *Alexander Pope, The Rape of the Lock and other Poems*, Geoffrey Tillotson, ed. 1940, third edition 1962.

John Press. *The Chequer'd Shade*. 1958.

John Press. *The Fire and the Fountain*. 1955.

George Puttenham. *The Arte of English Poesie*, Gladys D. Willcock and Alice Walker, eds. 1936.

Sir W. Ralegh. *The Poems of Sir Walter Ralegh*, Agnes Latham, ed. 1951.

W. Shakespeare. *King Henry V*, J. H. Walker, ed. 1954.

W. Shakespeare. *Twelfth Night*, Morton Luce, ed. 1906.

Sir P. Sidney. *An Apology for Poetry*, Geoffrey Shepherd, ed. 1965.

Alfred Tennyson. *Poetical Works*, Oxford Standard Authors. 1953, reprinted 1959.

M. P. Tilley. *A Dictionary of the Proverbs in England in the Sixteenth and Seventeenth Centuries*. 1950.

E. M. W. Tillyard. *The Elizabethan World Picture*. 1943, fourth impression 1948.

Rosemond Tuve. *Elizabeth and Metaphysical Imagery*. 1947, Phoenix edition 1961.

Henry Vaughan. *Poetry and Selected Prose*, L. C. Martin, ed. 1963.

T. K. Whipple. *Martial and the English Epigram from Sir Thomas Wyatt to Ben Jonson*. 1925.

Oscar Wilde. *Plays, Prose Writings, and Poems*, Everyman's edition 1930, reprinted 1945.

George Williamson. *The Donne Tradition*. 1930.

George Williamson. *The Proper Wit of Poetry*. 1961.

Edmund Wilson. *Axel's Castle*. 1931.

Edgar Wind. *Pagan Mysteries in the Renaissance*. 1958.

Sir T. Wyatt. *Collected Poems of Sir Thomas Wyatt*, Kenneth Muir, ed. 1949, paperback edition 1963.

W. B. Yeats. *Collected Poems*. 1950.

W. B. Yeats. *The Letters of W. B. Yeats*, Allan Wade, ed. 1954.

W. B. Yeats. *The Variorum Edition of the Poems of W. B. Yeats*, Peter Allt and Russell K. Alspach, eds. 1957, reprinted 1965.

Index